"Deep Within I knew He Wasn't For ME... Ignoring the Red Flags"

By

Tanicia

"Shamay Speaks"

Currie

Published by Shamay Speaks

www.ShamaySpeaks.com

Book cover designed by Shauny B with KnockSmith Productions
http://www.knocksmithmagazine.com/

Back Cover photo taken by Nicole Barton
http://www.nicolebartonphotography.com/

Make-up for the photo by Silvina Lopez with Mac Make up
(Antioch, Ca)

Shamay Speaks Logo designed by BJ "Photo B" Colston
(Sacramento, Ca)

Printed in the United States of America
ISBN: 978-0-9966729-0-0

Dedication

I dedicate this book to all the women who have made bad choices in relationships for whatever reason. I also dedicate this book to the single mother's out there who never give up on their goals.

4

Table of Contents

Part III

Part IV

Acknowledgements

I would like to take this time to thank GOD because without him, nothing is possible; therefore, this is his will. I dedicate this book to every person who has come and gone out of my life and left a lesson for me. My true dedication for this book is the best blessing ever, my daughter Laniyah. My daughter was the best blessing from the biggest lesson but I would go through it 100 times again just to have her. Laniyah, you are my breath, my light, my happiness, my EVERYTHING. Mommy loves you more than anything. Thank you for changing me for the better, my honeybunn. I also dedicate this book to my uncle Steven Avilla who passed February 28, 2015. Uncle you have always had the best influence on me and I know you are shining down on me daily. I will do what your last words were by keeping myself around like-minded people. I truly thank my grandmother Betty Conner, for she is the best woman in my life. Big Ma, you allowed me to get my life back on track and you have always been there for me without judgment. You said to me the other day that a lot of people do not talk "my language," and that means a lot to me. What you said to me shows me that I am on the right path with changing my mindset and growing personally. You are a blessing to so many!

I thank my best friend of 20+ years, Shana, you have always been there. You are a sister, more than a friend. You always gave me a listening ear and I trust you with my life. Shana, where would I be without your friendship? Thank you for speaking up for me ☺. Telling me no when I needed to hear it. I thank my cousins, Eshe' and Akilah Satcher, we are family but also best friends. Family 1st! I love you guys! Thanks to all my true friends, I have a list but you all know who you are! Shout out to one of my best friends Jimmy for keeping my nails fresh and being there especially during my last heart surgery. I thank my best friend Santiago for always being there for me when I needed help especially car problems; I know I can always count on you. I have some awesome friends. I love you all!

I want to take this time to thank my struggles because without them, how would I have learned? Yes, it could have been an easier way to learn but this is the way GOD saw fit for me to get it right. This is just the beginning of this success journey and I truly appreciate those who rode with me; especially when Cause N' A Stir Entertainment came about. Shout out to my Broken Wheel family and BJ "Photo B" Colston for the love and support over the years.

I also thank my support system: Linda and Reggie Turner, My mom, Deena Avilla, Tierra, Ariel, Dezjanae, Cashanay, Shannon, and anyone who helped me with my baby when I needed to work on my goals. I also want to thank my friend, Niya Trapps, who never let me forgot about writing my book over the years. Thanks to my girl Gina, and my cousin Jessica for getting my wheels spinning again. I also thank my sister, Marie Avilla, who gets on my LAST nerve but is always in the front row to support me. Thanks to my brothers, Dennis and James. I love you guys even though you drive me crazy!

I truly thank all the women who contributed their stories to this book. You are bold, courageous, and inspiring. You guys believed in me but you were also willing to help other women learn from your stories. Our stories will help other women and even if we help one woman, our goal is accomplished. You guys ROCK!

Thank you to my coach, Sheya Chisenga, I appreciate you never giving up on me and providing all the motivation to keep me focused. I love being around a group of amazing like-minded passionate women. You rock! You are headed to the top!

I definitely want to thank my business partners, Danae Braggs & Shaun "Shauny B" Smith for working with me. I appreciate the friendship and the contribution we each make to assist each other's success. Shaun, thank you so much for the book cover and everything you have done for my success. Knocksmith Magazine to the top! Anything is achievable! We are living proof!

Shout out to Nicole Barton for the great photos and Silvina L from Mac in Antioch for the beautiful look for my book cover shoot.

I thank everyone who supports me through kind words, sharing my Facebook and Youtube videos/posts, and just believing in me. Shout out to James Standifer and Chasity Toney for always supporting me with your kind words of encouragement, always sharing my videos/posts, attending my events, and just being supportive.

To everyone I love in heaven, I know you're all looking over me as guardian angels. I miss and love you all!

God guide me as it is YOUR WILL.

Introduction

By
Tanicia "Shamay Speaks" Currie

Let me start by saying, this book is not intended to man bash at all because ultimately we choose who we date. Dating! When I say that word, what comes to mind especially if you are single? I think that a lot of women may roll their eyes and think of the bad experiences they may have had that led them to being single now. Have you ever dated someone and later, like way later, it hits you that this is exactly what you said you didn't want in a relationship? Then you wonder why you didn't realize it and take action earlier. Well, what I have found after dating for 16 years, is that I was never dating someone that represented my CORE VALUES of what I envisioned for myself in a relationship. I learned I was never true to my core values. I did the opposite of what I wanted within my core. Let me break this down for you - according to the Webster's dictionary, the definition of core is "the central part or most important part of something." For me, my core would be my heart. In my CORE, I knew I wanted the best and never wanted to settle. Growing up, I always wanted to defy the odds like I wanted to be married before I had children and I tried hard to wait. I waited because I wanted a family and I wanted the family unit I never really saw with my parents. I had gotten pregnant at 17 and had a miscarriage. After the miscarriage, I vowed to wait until I was married to have a child. My core values were to wait and not because my family instilled those values in me. I wanted so bad to NOT be like everyone else and I didn't want to be a "Baby Mama".

Every time, especially in my mid 20's when I got hit with the "When are you going to have kids?"question; I'd always reply with, "When I get married." I made it all the way to 30 without having a child even though I had a couple long term relationships that were over four years long. Those long term relationships were nothing to brag about to say the least. There are so many lessons that I could tell you I learned just from dating but for this book, I want to focus on being more aware of red flags and following our CORE values as women. I want to briefly tell you all a little about how I learned, early on, the hard way that my CORE were not being fulfilled. I definitely want you all to understand what it took me to REALLY understand - I never lived up to my CORE values I envisioned for myself and why that needed to change. Why it took me 16 years, dead end toxic relationships, and becoming a single mother; to realize it. When I truly sit back and really reflect on my encounter with men and relationships, I realize I never really had true LOVE. I truly do not feel my perception of love was any where near what it really is. I started dating and having sex at a very young age, and I was one of those girls who no one ever talked to them about sex. I lost my virginity at 14½ while knowing nothing about sex. From having sex at such a young age and knowing nothing about it, I feel that it played a part in my false illusion of what love is. I truly feel the younger you become sexually active, the more issues you have when determining what love means to you in relationships. The younger you are, the harder it can be to separate lust from love especially when it comes to having standards and boundaries. At such a young age and having separated parents, I didn't know what a happy, healthy relationship was. My father was addicted to drugs and in and out of prison, so my father wasn't around consistently to show me about men. I honestly can't remember a time when I can say, wow my parents truly expressed love for each other. I think my mom wanted to save my father from himself and his addiction. In trying to save him, she may have forgotten about her own wants and needs like many women have. When you have parents who do not model a healthy relationship or even discuss relationships or sex with you; how do you know what a healthy or unhealthy relationship is? Even today, I still don't know what kind of love my parents really shared for each other during their relationship; I assume it wasn't the best because even at my baby shower for my daughter, my father wouldn't even take a picture with my mother and me. My parents broke up when I was 11, I assume, because my mother had another child with another man while my father was in jail. My father went to rehab after this and left my mother for whatever reasons, but as I said I guess it was because of the birth of my brother. It is crazy to me that he left being that he was in and out of prison pretty much their whole relationship. Even though two wrongs don't make a right, I don't blame my mother for dating someone else but what can a man expect when he is never there for his woman and children; however, I am glad they made me. The sad reality is a lot of our parents didn't have guidance themselves so as the saying goes, "If they knew better, they'd do better." I have one older sister and two younger brothers, one of whom I share a father with. We have all taken different paths in life, and I truly think a lack of guidance is to blame. At that point, I had never seen a healthy relationship outside of my paternal grandparents, who were married over 50 years, and my paternal great grandparents who were married over 75 years. So as far as knowing how important saving myself was or how important my body is, etc, I knew nothing. I was 14 ½ when I started dating or messing around, shall I say, so I was so clueless. I went to high school. 9th grade was cool and I was semi on track. My childhood friend introduced me to DB, a star football player at the high school. Even though I lost my virginity to him at 14 and we were never officially together, we remained great friends. My life went out of control from 14 ½ - 16, I was smoking, drinking, and

15

hanging in the streets. I met Deon when I was 16 while working at a fast food place. I thought wow this time I got a "real" boyfriend. It started off good, but when I met him I was in the middle of changing homes and high schools. My father was slapped with child support and all of a sudden he wanted custody, so I had to move in with him. I really feel for my mom because she kind of got left in the wind after he got off drugs but then again, women need to know when it's time to walk away. So when I started dating Deon, it was cool until all the real crazy drama started. This was my "real" relationship right? And it lasted from age 16- 20 ½. I was young but due to my lack of guidance and my drive to be independent, I put myself in an adult relationship that I was not ready for. This relationship was so crazy and it ended with the beginning of me losing myself and ignoring my core values. You'll read about this in the "Young and Misguided" chapter. That relationship was truly the beginning of me making poor decisions when entering relationships.

After this relationship, I was single for about 8 months but was still dating or having sex shall I say. With that being said, I never took the time to work on me. Right after this relationship I met a man who was amazing and was on the right track in life. He was everything I wanted. He was employed, had a car, and his own place. I latched onto him easily and he was fine but he never wanted titles. I could never figure out why because our situation was good and we really enjoyed each others company. Since he and I were not official, I kept my options open. He and I remained close off and on. Shortly after this, I met a man who I liked just because of his pretty eyes and personality. I felt I was a little damaged before I met him from my past relationship so I guess drama was normal to me or I had low self-esteem; moreover, I stayed in this unhealthy relationship for over four years but I will leave the details for the chapter "I Guess It Was Those Eyes."

After those four years in which I had drama still, I met the man who would make me a mother at 30. Out of everything that I had experienced in dating and relationships, becoming a single mom would be the thing that would pull my blinders off and fully reveal that I was not following my core values. I went through so much from 2011-2014, including having my second open heart surgery at just age 29. I feel like it was God telling me that now was the time to finish the book I started in 2006. I decided to put this book together because over the years one thing I realized was that many women of all ages from all walks of life have a story about a dating or relationship experience; that can only be summed up as a learning experience. I, most importantly, feel that mistakes can only be learned from if you realize what signs you missed as well as your own faults.

I just wanted to provide you with a little insight as to how I got to this point. Please enjoy the book. ☺

Disclaimer

The views and/or opinions in this book do not reflect the views and/or opinions of each of the women whose stories are featured.

Part I

By: Shamay Speaks

Disclaimer: I, in no way, shape, or form, neither claim to be a love doctor nor do I have the cure for heartache. I cannot tell you exactly what true love is but I can tell you what it is NOT! I am simply applying my personal knowledge, experiences, and observations to help others. I am in no way judging other women. I hope that some women can learn from this book so it will help guide them in a different direction besides heartbreak which is sometimes evitable.

Chapter 1

"YOUNG AND MISGUIDED BUT THE BEGINNING OF LOSING ME"

By

Shamay Speaks

Age 33

Bay Area, California

You may see why I titled this introduction chapter "Young and Misguided but the Beginning of Losing Me," but here's how my very first "real" relationship went. Our first "real" relationship can definitely shape our future relationships. I met Deon the day after I turned 16 while working at McDonald's. He was in my line staring at me and we exchanged numbers after I took his order. We started hanging out and we hit it off. This was officially my first real boyfriend even though I had a couple "friends," and I was not a virgin. Deon and I would hang out after school at his house while his parents were at work, so we were able to spend a lot of time together. I really liked his family and they liked me. Well things were going nice with our young love but I was going through some changes in my family like changing from living with my Mother to my Father gaining custody in a bitter battle. I always had an independent attitude on life. So I always wanted to work and be able to have the freedom to do what I wanted. I worked enough to buy my first car, so I was able to drive to my boyfriends after school or cut school ☺ During my household transitions, I changed schools and started a friendship with another guy. I ended up breaking up with Deon for really no good reason but I told him I wanted to date others; needless to say, things with the other guy didn't work out and I wanted Deon back. It's probably safe to say the grass was not greener on the other side but I was only 16. Deon really was my first REAL boyfriend. He really loved me or what I assumed was love from my young experience. I never experienced "Love" until him but I broke his heart. We got back together and that's when I started getting my share of drama, real drama at 17. I guess he resented me breaking up with him but he never told me; yet, he sure showed me. During our 4½ year relationship (age 16 to 21), I had a miscarriage and I was cheated on many times. I remember the first time he cheated on me, for some reason I felt I gave him a pass (Red Flag) because I had hurt him before even though I was never intimate with the other guy. When I found out, I was talking to him on a pay phone, about to get on the bus and head to work. The bus ride was about 15 minutes and by the time I got to work; he was in the lobby waiting for me. He was saying he was sorry and that they only had "oral sex." In my young mind "oral sex" wasn't as bad as "real cheating," right? This way of thinking was definitely that of an inexperienced, young minded young lady. I later found out that it was more than oral sex of course. The girl that he cheated with was nowhere near being similar to me, if you get what I'm saying. I say that to say that I realized at a young age that men don't only cheat for looks. The girl he cheated with assumed that she was in a relationship with him because they had messed around once. This girl worked at the local Wal-Mart and I would see her. This girl would have the nerve to come up and speak to me as if we were BFF's or something. I guess him telling her that he was working it out with his girlfriend wasn't enough for her. She would call him every time she saw me. So the drama with this girl continued. I also had my new car keyed, tires slashed, and "F**k you" wrote on my door by this girl. So I guess you would call this a girl scorned because we were teenagers so it wouldn't' be a woman scorned. After this drama, things started to get bad little by little, I found out I was pregnant at 17. I ended up having a miscarriage which was quite an ordeal. I had only told my mother I was pregnant even though I lived with my father. My father only found out because I had bad complications from the miscarriage and they had to call him because I was underage. The relationship continued to go downhill and for whatever reason, I wanted to cling to it. We eventually started fighting a lot and I had my first experience with domestic violence. (Big Red Flag) This relationship definitely didn't leave me in a good mental state for future relationships. I am sure if you asked me then why I put up with things, I probably would have said, "Because I love him." I think rationalizing other people's bad behavior can serve as a big red flag also. In reality, I absolutely never knew what love was and I was never talked to about sex; furthermore, how would I know that sex doesn't turn into love or what "love" was. I remember thinking what am I doing but I was young and truly didn't have anyone telling me that this relationship was not healthy. It was love, right? How it lasted four years, I truly don't know. How would I know that drama isn't love? I did some crazy things over this man, and I realize I semi lost myself. Losing myself in that relationship and being young caused me to act irrational for years. I am sure in my subconscious; I oddly thought crazy drama was healthy. Well that relationship ended with a physical fight and being forced to testify against my ex for domestic violence. I will say I did some crazy things because of the way I was treated and I wasn't perfect either. When I think back on all the crazy things I did, I feel I did them all for nothing. When reflecting, I think I did "psycho" things and wonder how I let myself go through that; however, love was the excuse right? Even though I lost myself in the land of love, I still tried my hardest to persevere in other aspects of life. Somewhere along this crazy time, I think I may have lost my core values before they could be shaped. As you can see, clearly this relationship wasn't modeling any CORE values but at 17 what are core values right? Especially when your parents haven't really shown you values or your value as a young woman. The sad part is no one, not even my mother, told me that the relationship wasn't for me. Now that I am more experienced and self-aware, I feel that there is no growth without some level of accountability for my part in this and what I put up with. After this, I stayed single for eight months but I dated. Now on to the next relationship, let's see how this goes.

Chapter 2

"I GUESS IT WAS THOSE EYES"

By

Shamay Speaks

Age 32

Bay Area, California

Before I met, well let's call him Mr. Blue, I had just got out of my first "real" relationship which was crazy to say the least. My cousins and I loved to attend comedy shows and go out to clubs, etc. One comedy show featured Arnez J and it was such a fun night. We sat up front and right when the show started, in walked a group of young men who sat right across from us. The comedian started talking about one of the guys in the group, like how he had a big head, etc. By the comedian doing this, which is hilarious, made my attention focus on this handsome man. After the show, he approached me and I saw his lovely Blue eyes. I always said I'd love to have a baby with Blue eyes so he was right up my alley. Now I was 20 at the time, so yes my thinking was a little shallow. Blue eyes definitely have nothing to do with a man's character. After the comedy show, we all went out to eat and his group sat with us. We got to chat for a while so I felt he was a cool dude besides, his Blue eyes were the best right? He explained to me that he had recently got out of prison for white collar crimes so I guess in my mind, it wasn't so bad. I've had family in jail for worse, so I'm thinking it wasn't a violent crime so it wasn't that bad. At the time, I wasn't really looking for a serious relationship because I was young and having fun with my fake ID. (hehe) After that day, we began to talk and text, that's when texting first was starting to become the popular way to communicate. He was funny, down to earth, and for some reason he was interesting. After dating for almost a month, he told me he had a friend who helped him while he was in jail and she was the one who paid for the phone he had. (Major Red Flag #1) I didn't think much because he was with me all the time and I didn't have any reason to not trust him yet! Mr. Blue loved nice things and I guess it was because he was fancy to that lifestyle before he went to prison. One day we went to the mall and he purchased some Jordan's, and I was thinking who the hell spends $200.00 on shoes? Then a couple days later, he comes to my house with a brand new pair of Jordan's which are the exact same ones he bought two days prior. I'm thinking that's odd, and he says he's going to return the other pair he bought. He says his friend bought the new pair for him and I am thinking what friend buys $200.00 shoes for anyone. (Major Red Flag #2) His main claim was he didn't ask her to do the things she did but in my young shallow mind; I thought whatever. We discussed how I felt about it and he made it clear that he didn't mess with her like that. At this time, we still were not official so I didn't make a big fuss; besides, I was still talking to another guy off and on. The other guy and I were not physical while I was dating Mr. Blue. We dated for about five months before we became official. He got a job close to where I lived, so he moved in with me and we became "official." Well, about two weeks after he moved in, he comes home looking all stressed. I am sitting at my computer doing college work and out of nowhere, he says, "She said she's pregnant." I stopped in my tracks, looking dumbfounded and thinking who the hell you talking about because I dam sure wasn't pregnant. When he says who, now her buying the shoes totally makes sense. (Major Red Flag #3) He says she did it on purpose because she knew he was putting distance between them because he wanted to be with me. He says he didn't want to mistreat her because of all she had done

26

for him but he never wanted a relationship with her: however, I'm sure that's not what he told her. That moment should have been the biggest red flag but I rationalized it in my mind as well we were not technically together when she got pregnant; so he didn't cheat, right? This is really when the true rollercoaster began. We lived in a city an hour away from her but, low and behold; I was going to be moving to her city to attend college the following year. I had college plans before I met him. You would think my educated self would have known better and been more in tune with the red flags. I was just 21 and still learning a lot especially about "love." For some odd reason, I didn't pay the pregnancy much mind because I felt he wanted me and was with me. He was constantly having issues because he says she wanted him and she was mad he wasn't with her, etc. Now remember, I said I didn't want to date men with kids, well now I was in this situation, so there went following my core values. It was definitely the true definition of baby mama drama but, I don't want to spend too much time on that portion of it; needless to say, she and I are friends now. A year later, he and I ended up moving to the city where I was getting ready to attend the university and where his future child's mother resided. She had their daughter a month after we moved there and I remember that day. I remember the day she had the baby, I was just stuck. I felt a real reality brick hit me because all this time before it didn't seem so real. It probably didn't seem as real either because the real drama hadn't began yet. As for my relationship, I felt things were okay because remember he didn't technically cheat on me when he got her pregnant because we were not together. I obviously continued to rationalize his behavior. He was a very charismatic man so women loved him and those eyes. He wasn't the kind of man to stay out all night or anything but he was a mess. There were so many incidents that I am sure as a type this, I will start having flashbacks. The first big incident was, one night I had a friend call me and tell me that she had seen him at a happy hour with another woman. He was supposedly with a friend but how do you have female friends that your live-in girlfriend knows nothing about. (Red Flag #4) I started going through his phone and finding all kinds of numbers, texts from exes and other women, etc. He would even hide women's number under his friend's names. I began to have a strong distrust towards him but I loved his mother and his family while beginning to form a bond with his child. We also had an amazing sex life or lust life shall I say. I supported him through all the custody court issues, and I was just always there for him. I probably was too involved and too supportive. He had his sweet times and he was very giving but very selfish with the way he thought about things. I think I always deep down thought he would change. I was definitely the hold it down bread winner in this relationship. He was a gambler and won a lot so he loved to dress the best and show out, and he was very materialistic. He loved to impress people especially women and it was like he got a high from it. I became very jealous and was always accusing him because I would always find something. As they say, if you seek you shall find. The question is if you find something, will it really change anything if you are already rationalizing red flag behavior? I felt lost but I guess his drama and college kept me busy. During our relationship, his mother passed away so that took a toll on him also. His mother was a great woman but his father was a total player. What was so crazy about it was that he resented how his father treated his mother yet he turned out the same way. One day I saw a message in his phone from a chick mentioning some shoes she had bought for his daughter and I was livid. (Red Flag) He insisted she was his friend from his home town but my neighbor told me that a chick in a grey car had came to my house while I was at work. I guess in my mind, my neighbor never said that they went in my house so I slightly dismissed it. I think at this point in my life was when I really learned that women do not care if you have someone, they will still mess around with you. It may sound naïve but out of all the instances when I caught him being disloyal, I never heard or seen him not "claim" me. It's like he was an honest cheater at least to them right. As our relationship went further downhill, I began to lose myself more and more. I no longer cared what my core values were for a relationship but I was a fighter; I fought for anything I wanted even if it wasn't good for me like I had something to prove.

Just to give a glimpse into how lost I was I found this journal entry I wrote almost nine years ago, after I had been with Mr. Blue for almost a year and a half.

Boy! What a life I had. I don't think I can even point out a time when I have been happy in my life. I can't even trust the one's I love; I love Mr. Blue with all my heart. I gave him my all but that wasn't enough, and I guess I was living in fairytale land thinking that he was the one for me. I don't know how to not feel like I'm stupid. I feel like I have messed up in giving my heart to the wrong people, I'm not strong enough for this. I'm losing my mind, my mind is not together. I can't help but think I just wasted two years of my life, and I am attached to him, his baby, and his family. I worked out today that was a good thing but I was so unfocused I may not keep that up. I don't know where to begin because my broken heart is controlling my feelings. I need to move on to something more, but it's so hard to do that. I don't know where to start, so I came home today and told myself that I was gonna trust him till' he proved me wrong. I wanted it to be like that so bad but I guess not. I don't know how to change. Since I was 16, I have been hurt every time I put my heart into someone; so I don't know where that will end. Hopefully, I will learn my lesson this time and look at it as a big learning

29

experience. I'm so stuck, I can't work because the day will start out fine but once the situation crosses my mind, I lose focus. I guess there's a thousand times I can point to where I went wrong, I messed up big time. The first time I had a bad feeling about the relationship, I should have left. When Lisa got pregnant, I should have left, but I have no clue why I stuck around! Maybe it was stupid me that thought I can trust someone, and maybe I messed up and thought he would respect me because I been there for him so much. But I'm learning no matter what I do for someone, out of the kindness of my heart, it doesn't matter because maybe that's all they wanted me for. I can't even think about where I go from here. I love him like no other, but I know he doesn't feel the same about me. That hurts real bad. I guess the fact that he wouldn't give me an anniversary wasn't a big enough hint to my stupid ass. Maybe I should have left him alone when he put hands on me, but I loved him so much that I thought it was my fault and I caused it. I should place the blame on myself for not protecting my feelings from this. I have to know where to change but I have no clue. I don't know where my trust for people came from but I wish I had a mom and dad who showed me the way. I wanted so much for myself, but I have the hardest time getting there. I messed up in school; I had a suppose-to-be man, who didn't care about me. He only cared about what I did for him in the long run. My self-esteem is so bad that I don't even know where to begin. I know I am a pretty girl, but I am not confident with myself. I have wasted time being faithful to one man, but loyalty doesn't count for nothing. I need counseling because I can't deal with these kinds of problems myself. I'm 21 and I can't help but feel that I have not succeeded in life. I feel like a big failure. I am finding that I lack self-discipline and self-control.

Wow, is probably what you are saying about that. I shock myself reading it but I have come a long way. All I knew about relationships was cheating and pure drama. I feel like, to some degree, I got so used to it that constant drama was normal; not realizing how mentally unhealthy it was. He would tell me things like, "I wish I could get everything out of my system and preserve you because I want to marry you." "I'll never find another girl to do everything you do with and for me." I guess in my mind, I took that as I am going to eventually change for you. We had a total love and hate relationship and I totally loved his child too. When it was good, it was great, but when it was bad it was BAD. The bond and love I had established for his daughter and his family was partly why I stayed. I think I also stayed because of the fear and leaving and starting over. We fought a lot sometimes physical fighting. There were so many times, I called or texted women, getting the same reply about his disloyal behavior. I think at times, I would be mad at them as if he wasn't the true cause. Reality was your man's loyalty lies with him not another woman and she really doesn't owe you anything. Towards the end of our tumultuous relationship, I had him sign me off the lease of my own apartment because even though I stuck around; I knew the end was near. At one point towards the end of relationship, he had damaged my car window and refused to pay to fix it. I ended up suing him in small claims court and we ended up going on Judge Joe Brown. That adventure was pretty interesting and I am sure you're thinking its crazy.... It was! During this time I was still losing myself. One of the final straws was I discovered he took a woman who lived in our apartment complex out to dinner. Sad thing is, this woman knew he lived with his girlfriend. I really loved this man but for some reason I didn't really let go even after this. One day shortly after he came home, and I had half the U-haul packed. I was moving alone to the place him and I was suppose to move to. I left being unemployed with $5000.00 to my name and my rent was

31

$860.00/month. My financial situation didn't matter because I just needed to leave period for my sanity. He started saying why did I leave, he was sorry, and he wanted me to move back. At this point it had been over 4 years of being together and I had deep love, or what I thought was love for him. After I moved I was still visiting him and being intimate with him. I guess, in my mind, I let go but not all the way. There is much more to this story but, needless to say, I feel I became a broken woman from this and the relationship before this. I even got in a physical altercation with the woman he took out to eat. She truly taught me that women can be very scandalous and care less if they know you have a woman already. I will say that wasn't even the final straw which is odd after everything that happened during this toxic relationship. I had found out something about another woman he had slept with, so I called to tell him what I found out and then went to his house. I was livid when I called him. I confronted him and of course, he denied it but I had proof of it being fact. After I left his house that night, I called him one last time to tell him about himself. When he answered the phone, he said, "You on your way back?" Those words literally echoed in my ear all the way home. I truly don't know what hit me at that moment but it felt like a bright light shined in my face, like the BIGGEST light bulb turned on. After everything he did to me and what I allowed, those words hit me like a ton of bricks. I think what really hit me was this man, who I loved and gave my all to, yet who treated me like dirt; felt like he was invincible with me. After hearing those words that had cut so deep, it dawned on me that he felt as if I would never leave him and as if I wasn't going anywhere. The worse part was coming to the harsh realization of what I had allowed and how much this toxic relationship consumed me. After that day, I never let him touch me again. I feel like it was a sign from God. After all he did, which I could write a novel about, those simple words could end it all. I think back especially about the baby mother situation and think, if she only knew what I went through with him; she would have never wanted him anyways. I probably saved her the worst headache of her life. The blessing is her and I have become friends. It's crazy how things can change and become a friendship after removing the problem. 7 years later and having a child now, I see some deja-vu from what I have experienced now being a single mom. Never say never because I am now in her shoes. I now know exactly what she went through, and I wouldn't wish it on anyone. God will show you that you can go through things you thought wouldn't happen. Anyways, this truly was one of those relationships that I am sure that, now in my 30's, if my friend was going through the mess I went through; I may not want any part of it because it was always negative. I learned lust does not equal love and it just takes you on an emotional rollercoaster. I don't think I ever really had a good perception of healthy relationships and neither did he. It was like it has been said by Iyanla Vanzant, a broken man with a broken woman. I had it together as far as being a college graduate and being totally independent but inside I was a broken woman. During that relationship, I did have a few people ask me what are you doing with him. They said it in an "I know you're smarter than that," way. Maybe that was a red flag right, one of many I clearly ignored. This was one of those relationships, like many, I had to leave him alone because he would have continued this toxic pattern. I have found that for whatever reason, many men like this will not leave the woman. The woman has to grow and obtain some self-awareness to learn this isn't a good relationship for her which is what I had to do. I don't want to fully bash him because there is good in everyone and he was a good person, just not a good man in relationships. He was used to a lifestyle that he didn't want to let go no matter what the cost. I learned that some men are good people, just not good at being loyal and monogamous in relationships and it's sad but true in my opinion. I could sit and have regrets but instead I rather determine how I can do things

33

different in the future. I had to do a lot of growing. I was growing and getting back on track with life and my goals. After this relationship I stayed single for 4 years but I dated, I just didn't want a relationship. Anytime I dated anyone and they presented ANY thing that made me flash back to this relationship, I left it alone. I was growing slowly but surely. I learned so much right? But then I met Shaun. ("The Lives He Lived" Chapter)

Chapter 3

"THE LIVES HE LIVED"

By

Shamay Speaks

Age 33

Bay Area, California

I wanted to title this story "The Liar by Omission," but I decided on "The Lives He Lived." Let me break that down a little bit. The "The Liar by Omission" man is the man who usually lives so many lives and tells so many lies that he actually believes them because he lives them on a daily basis. He is very charismatic and quite charming and down to earth. Everyone in town that knows him would describe him as a very cool person. If you want a movie that puts this in perspective for you watch, "The Other Woman" featuring Cameron Diaz. Remember these type of men are stars in their own movies and they bring along blind female co-stars, if you get what I mean.

I had been single for almost four years but of course I dated a few within that time period. I had been in recovery from my second open heart surgery so dating anyone was not on my mind. One random night in late October 2011, my cousin texted me and asked did I want some company. I thought about it and said why not. The evening came and he arrived with my cousin's friend. We'll call him Shaun. Shaun and I seem to hit it off instantly. During that night we drove to the store together and had a long talk and the discussion included men living double lives. He said it wasn't cool, etc. Note: there was a Beyoncé' CD in the car (should have been the 1st Red flag) but he said it was his sisters because she had used his car. Now a while ago, because I didn't want to carry baggage, I decided I was going to trust someone until they proved me wrong. From our conversation, I really liked him. Now his story went like this, he was recently single. He had been in a 13 year off/on relationship and he had 2 sons. He stated his ex was partially moved out and their lease was ending. We exchanged numbers that evening and a few days later, he texted me. We chatted through text and planned a date. After that day, I asked a few people that knew him, what he was about. I received all good reviews and they all stated he was single. We went on our first date and he was such a gentlemen. He opened car doors and all, and I thought he's such a gentlemen. We hit it off. We continued to chat and planned the second date and we were intimate on this second date. The intimacy was amazing and it seemed like he hadn't had sex in a while; moreover, why I felt he wasn't seeing anyone. Now Shaun was a Mechanic so I knew that when I texted he couldn't always reply right away so I never made a fuss about his late replies. Plus, he literally worked at the shop a block from my grandmother's house. During the time we dated I lived in Sacramento which was an hour away so, I would see him 2-4 times a week when I was in town visiting for business, etc. I hosted events at a nightclub so on the weekends I would be out very late. There would be times I wouldn't be able to see him because I was running my business but he would usually stay up late to see me. It would be late when we would spend time together due to my schedule so when he would doze off, I would totally understand that he was tired. I even gave him the nickname "Dozer" because he dozed off in front of me, from being tired from "work." There were a few times, I would text him goodnight, etc, and he would not reply. The next morning, he would usually say he fell asleep. (2nd Red flag) Remember, during the time we dated, I lived an hour away so I would only be in town two-four days at a time. When I was in town, we spent every free minute we could together. I would go see him at work and he would visit me all the time. Being that I always saw him when I wanted and at work, I never really thought about him seeing other women. We went on dates and all. Things were going good and after 2 months, he dropped the "L" word. He said I love you while we were texting one day. (3rd Red flag)When I saw the message I replied saying we would have to talk about that in person. A couple days later, we were hanging out and as we said our goodbyes, he said, "I love you and I can tell you in person." After he said it, he gave me the most sensual kiss, curled my toes. I never said it back because I was still a little thrown off but as time went on I started to feel the same. I hadn't had a serious relationship in a while so this felt so good to be in "love." At that point, we didn't have official labels but we knew where we stood or at least I thought we did. (4th Red flag) He would say things that would insinuate that we were in a relationship so I didn't worry much about it. Shaun's claim from day one was that he had just left that 13 year relationship, so I didn't care to rush him. (5th Red flag) I gave time because I know from my past; I remember how much time I needed after my last relationship. I believe, even more so now, that people should take time to work on themselves before getting into new relationships. Plus, I wasn't sure that I wanted a full relationship and felt I may need more time but I loved him. I met his mother a couple times and hung out with her, and she even mentioned us having kids. Things were still going good and for Christmas, he gave me a gold necklace with a heart and a key charm. He said it was because he has the key to my heart, and I thought it was the sweetest thing. Our friends and family used to make comments like you guys are so in love because he was so affectionate with me all the time, etc. Shaun and I even talked about having kids in the future. I didn't have any kids yet because I wanted marriage first. Shaun already had two kids, one estranged. After dating for three months, one morning he woke up late and said he had to leave to go visit his friend in jail. I thought that's odd, he never mentioned having a friend in jail. I didn't question it but definitely made a mental note of it. Right after that, I caught the flu and Shaun took off work to bring me soup and medicine. When I think back, those first 3 months were probably the honeymoon stage. Right before Valentine's Day, I started getting these harassing private number phone calls, up to 36 calls in one day. It got the point that I had to a file police report. Why would the person never say anything? I thought it could be anyone since my number was on thousands of event flyers yet it was extremely odd. My number has been public for years especially for business, etc. Long story short, these harassing calls went on every day for over three months. Note: Shaun's phone would always ring but he would say it was customers. I became really frustrated and had to confront Shaun because I knew only an upset woman would play these phone games. Only someone with too much time on her hands would be doing this. He claimed he was not dating anyone else and had no clue. Hmm, we'll get back to that later. (6th Red flag) Our relationship started to kind of change and I was out of town a little more dealing with family stuff as I was raising my teenage brother. It seemed like every time I felt we needed to spend more time, Shaun would always make time and make it up to me. I now realize he was very good at short term satisfaction. (7th Red flag) Even though I started to feel different, I loved him and the sex was the bomb. During mid-May, when I was starting to push away, we spent three great days together. Note: at this point since the shop closed, Shaun was a "Busy Mobile Mechanic." I was starting to move and Shaun promised to help but he "got stuck at work." (8th Red flag) After this, I decided I was done with him. I decided this, mainly because I felt something was off and those harassing calls were still going. I didn't see Shaun for a full month but he kept contacting me and asking me to talk to him. I refused because I wanted to leave him alone and I didn't see the point. On June 12, I officially moved to my hometown which is where he lived. Right before I moved there was an older woman who had added me on Facebook and I went through her profile pictures. I must have sent her a request so many months prior that I forgot because I didn't even remember sending it. I later found out that she had recently been released from jail. Interesting enough, when I discovered the release date, my calls abruptly stopped two weeks before that date; furthermore, until this day I still wonder who that was. The Facebook friend request was accepted about a week after my harassing calls finally stopped. As I looked through her profile pictures, I noticed a picture of her and Shaun from about a year prior. (9th Red flag) This is extremely odd because remember he was suppose to be in his previous 13 year relationship at the time of that picture. Although I was done with Shaun, the day I moved out there, he contacted me. He asked to see me and I was pretty done, but great sex didn't sound too bad. Don't judge me. We hung out and he spent the night, and he kept saying how much he missed and loved me. Little did I know everything was about to come together full circle and make sense but not total sense. After we woke up that next morning, I asked him who the woman was who added me on Facebook. He said it was a friend. (10th Red flag) I said, "Hmm, okay," but since I decided that I wasn't dating him anymore; I let it go. I thought it was over or so I thought. A week later, I am on Facebook and the first thing I see in my news feed is a picture of him and the older woman with the quote, "love is in the air." Keep in mind, Shaun was still relentlessly pursuing me. I looked at the comments on the picture, and even his mother commented, etc. I thought that was odd because his mom knew of me though she didn't know I stopped dealing with him. I immediately called Shaun to ask about this because I thought we were grown enough to be honest and we didn't have protected sex. I gave him three hours to call me back before I contacted this woman. One thing is, social media tells all and it's like a mini background check. I started to think well if this woman was around during his last relationship, she must have been a total side chick. (11th Red flag) This was also a sign that he must have been living double lives because he was in a 13 year relationship back then, right? But where did this woman come from? Well a week later, I found out I was pregnant. Imagine the shock I was in, even though I was done with him, learning he lied since day one then finding out I'm six weeks pregnant. It was too much especially since I didn't want kids until marriage and with what I just discovered. I could write a full book about my pregnancy but we'll save that for later. A month and a half later, after a nightmare month full of drama and extreme life changes, I discovered I wasn't the only one pregnant. (12th Red flag) This confirmed what I said earlier about the lives he lived. Note: the other woman pregnant was not the ex or the older woman from Facebook. So let's tally that up, he was living four lives that I discovered so far. Of course, he said he didn't know if it was his baby, the condom broke, and he was drunk blah blah. I was totally shocked by hearing of another baby but I was not shocked for long. About a month after I happen to be on Facebook and saw a picture of his car in my news feed; I guess a mutual Facebook friend of mine had commented on this picture. I clicked on the picture and what do you know, it was a woman's Facebook. I read the comments and that revealed yet another relationship so that now tallies five lives he was living. I guess the car he was driving was hers and she had also recently found out about the older woman in jail. Super long story short, he denied everything and said he still loved me. It was pretty laughable but being pregnant and dealing with all this, was no laughing matter. I had this precious little girl who was going to need me and I realized that he wasn't going to be more than what he was now. If he couldn't keep up with all these lives he lived, how could he be a father to these two babies coming? I knew that I did not want to be with him period. I was extremely disappointed in myself for dating him, for getting pregnant, but mostly for getting pregnant and not being able to have the family I always dreamed of. There were so many emotions I had to deal with; it made my pregnancy pretty stressful. I had to contain my stress because remember, I have a heart condition. Through all this, I discovered I needed to be accountable for my choices in this. I chose to be with him and I didn't take enough time to get to really know him. He put on an Oscar worthy act for months but like they say if it's too good to be true; it probably is. I got pregnant due to taking antibiotics which made my birth control ineffective; however, I could have used condoms. The harshest reality in this all was realizing my part in this, realizing that I wasn't being careful with my heart or life. Yes, I was single for 4 years prior to him, but I wasn't really following my heart when dating. Reflecting is something we all must do as women to realize what we could have done differently. Just because you enjoy someone's time, doesn't mean they are the one. Just because sex is good, doesn't mean you shouldn't protect your body and your heart. The rude awakening I had was that I had values yet I wasn't living by none of them. When you don't live your life aligned with your values, you're destined for failure especially in the love department. I told myself, I did not want to date anyone who wasn't established yet I continued to date him after he moved in with his mom. If you remember earlier in the story, I mentioned I left him alone for a month. I knew something was off but I should have followed my heart earlier on. I love my daughter and I would go through everything again just for her; however, I wouldn't wish this situation on my worst enemy. All those red flags I missed, added to my negative relationship experiences, made me realize I wasn't living up to my own values. He was my eye opener from God because God knew something had to wake me up for me to change. I truly feel that God showed me that he was going to give me the best blessing ever but not without giving me a life lesson. I had to do some extreme soul searching which I am still doing. It took all this plus my bad experiences, over the course of 14 years, to realize I didn't love myself enough. I allowed many things to occur that went against what I valued in a relationship which went against what I knew I was worth. I had been ignoring the messages God had been sending me. If I wanted a husband, why was I dating so carelessly? If I wanted marriage before children, why was I not being more careful? If I wanted real love, why didn't I give myself more time to get to know him before giving him my love? I learned that life will keep sending you messages that show you that you are not living right or show you that you do not love yourself enough. My bad dating choices were showing me that I was continuing to not make the right choices. It took for me to become a single mom which was one of my biggest fears, to realize that my actions didn't follow my heart or core values. God's biggest blessing turned to be my biggest lesson. My baby is such a blessing and I am happy to say her father and I are now great co-parents. He's not perfect but no one is. It's all about how you deal with it and having boundaries. I love that I was able to let things go for the best interest of my child because it can be challenging being mature while mending a broken heart. Her father made me learn me and what I wanted, so I thank him for that. I thank him for stepping up and being a father. Now his personal life is his issue but he's turned out to be a better father day by day. I pray for him daily that he will experience more and more personal growth each day. I thank God for pulling the blinders off my eyes which has helped me to learn to love me first. Yes, you have to go through things to learn sometimes, but if you do not love yourself first; you will never be happy with anyone. I learned it all starts with you!

PART II

This section includes seven stories from seven amazing women from all walks of life who have been in relationships that presented red flags; but may have chosen to overlook them. We can all learn something from one another.

Chapter 4

"I DID EVERYTHING I NEEDED TO DO TO GET A WOMAN LIKE YOU!"

By

Robin Robinson-Myhand

Age 50+

Sacramento, CA

Walter and I had met in the late 70's or early 80's at William Land Park. It was a casual conversation and from time to time we would run into each other over the years. He needed to do some growing up so I never put much into the few times I had seen him around town. He was always polite.

I had been on my first cruise in 1992 to the Caribbean and had met someone from St. Lucia. He worked on the cruise ship and kept in touch with me after the cruise was over. I found him attractive and definitely different than the men I was meeting in Sacramento. He had made arrangements for me to come to Florida and to stay at the Ramada Inn. I verified that I actually had a room reserved for me and was getting ready to schedule my flight when he had to return to the cruise ship earlier than expected. I received a phone call and he stated that this was not the kind of life that he wanted and he didn't want to put me through this again. With him working on the cruise line there would be more disappointments and he felt I deserved better.

A few weeks later, I came home and my apartment manager tells me that a very handsome and well-dressed man had come by inquiring about me and had left his business card and wanted me to contact him. I looked at the card and it was Walter Butler. He was a supervisor with the State of California. On the back of the card was his home and cell phone number. In 1993, very few people had cell phones.

A few days later my manager said that he had come by again to see if I had gotten his card and he asked me if I had called him. I had not. My manager stated "the man seems very interested. You're single, so what's the problem? Give him a call."

I gave him a call and we caught up. He was definitely a more mature person than what I had remembered. He asked if he could take me to dinner and I agreed to meet him. He did not know what apartment I lived in just the apartment complex. Walter lived across the street from me and had seen me a few times so he decided to make contact.

We had a nice dinner. Light conversation and I let him know that I had just had a letdown and wasn't all that interested in a serious relationship. He was cool with that and stated we could just have a friendly relationship. For a few months that was all it was. He would call and we would talk and go out from time to time. During this time he told me about his childhood, his mistakes, failed marriage and two children.

Walter was born in Lafayette Louisiana and was raised by his grandmother in Houston Texas. He was the oldest child. His mother had him very young and married his father because she was pregnant. His grandmother took care of him and raised him. The family wanted him to come back to Lafayette and work in the family business so in his senior year of high school he went back to Lafayette and graduated from Lafayette High School. He was very resentful of his parents because he really didn't know them or his other siblings very well and wanted to stay in Houston with his grandmother. He always referred to his grandmother with love and admiration.

He went into the Air Force and that is how he eventually came to Sacramento. He met someone and she got pregnant. Once the child was born he suspected that the child was not his. She had named the child after him but their relationship ended and there was no relationship with her or the child. He moved on and had not contact with her or the child since he was few months old. He did not know if she lived in Sacramento or not.

He then became involved with another woman and she became pregnant. He realized very early on that she was crazy and they went their separate ways. He had a relationship with his son but had had a lot of grief with the mother. Years later he was in another relationship and he had a daughter with another woman. He was in contact with her and his daughter and things were cordial. She had moved to Seattle Washington and he had not seen his daughter in a few months but he did talk to her on a regular basis. She was into skating and he had few videos of her skating and she wanted to compete. At this time his son was 19 and his daughter was 12 or 13 I believe. He stated that he was paying child support for her and his son had lived with him for a year due to problems with his mom. His son was not with his grandmother and working.

He married a woman named Sherry and they were married for five years. She had two children and he was in touch with them. There were no problems with her children but her actions caused a bankruptcy; therefore, problems in their relationship. He had been divorced for many years and had an interest in someone but wasn't sure how to let this person know. We talked about it and I gave him advice and told him to ask her out for lunch, let her know and see where it goes from there. Keep it light; don't put out a whole lot of money and time. About a week later he told me had a lunch date and was excited. I told him congratulations and wished him luck. While at work, I get a call that there is someone that wishes to see me. It was Walter Butler. I went outside and saw him. He had rose in his hand and gave it to me. He said he wanted to thank me for giving him the courage to pursue this woman. He asked to go with him to his car as he had brought a little gift and he wanted to know if he should give it to her or not. I went to the car and there was another rose. He also handed me a note. I said, "What does the note say". He said, "Open it". I opened it and it said "I thought you knew that it was always you". I was in shock. I was totally clueless. We began dating. He was always very thoughtful and consistent. He proudly introduced me to people and after 11 months he asked me to marry him. I accepted and we began to plan our wedding.

Christmas time was coming and he had plans to go to Houston and Louisiana to see his family. He asked if I would come to meet his family. I flew into Houston on Christmas day. I met an Aunt and his grandmother in Houston. They were both surprised and very pleased. He drove me around Houston and showed me where he went to school, played sports and where he and his grandmother used to stay when he was younger. I met a few cousins and then we went to Lafayette to meet his parents and siblings. When we arrived at his parents' house I was warmly received. People came from down the street and next door to see him. I found out that he had a nick name "Big Shot" and that's what a lot of people called him. I talked with this mother and father and even went to the neighborhood meat market with his father and he treated me to Boudin sausage since I had never had it before.

The next day Walter had walked to a cousin's house two blocks over from his parents. He called and wanted me to walk over and he would meet me half way. He told me that I would probably be approached by several men that were at the corner store. Tell them you are with Butler and they will leave you alone.

Sure enough I was approached and I told them I was with Butler and they backed off. I saw him coming around the corner and when they saw him these men became very respectful and even apologized to me. I was like wow, what's up with that? I just figured that the name must have respect in the neighborhood as they had lived there for so long.

We hung out with his cousins for a while. He discussed completing college with one of them and encouraged her to hang in there. Later at his parents' house I looked at old photos and met more members of the family. I liked the family and made a connection with his brother Martin who had promised to take me to Mardi

Gras one year as he went as often as he could and loved it. He knew what Balls to go to and had a place for us to stay. I was excited and felt comfortable with his family.

A few months after we returned I moved in with him as he had a bigger place and the rent was very reasonable. I was able to save money, plan a wedding and spend time getting to know him on a day to day basis. We worked through some things as we both were used to living with ourselves. He apologized with flowers, making me dinner or taking me to dinner. He took care of me when I was sick and everything was going along fine. The wedding plans were pretty stress free.

As the wedding approached he was very surprised that his mother, grandmother and brother were coming for the wedding due to the expense. A few weeks before the wedding he wanted to look at trucks. What? Why? He always wanted a truck. He had been promoted to a new position with the State and wanted another vehicle. The trucks he had in mind were too damn expensive and I thought that that had put that purchase on the back burner. Plus the wedding was coming up so why incur a new expense. One week before the wedding I am at work and he shows up at the job with the car dealer and a truck. A black Chevy truck with red pin stripes that is lowered had crush red interior and a chain link steering wheel. He needs my signature to get it because of his credit score. He will have the payments taken out of his check automatically but needs my help. I was furious. I allowed my coworkers and the sales person to talk me into it. The payment is coming out of his check and three women there had men who loved trucks. They all said. "He's a truck guy. Let him get it out of his system now. Once the gas bills start kicking his butt, he will get rid of it." I signed and the next day a huge bouquet of flowers was delivered to the office stating I love you and thank you. It was so big I just left it there for everyone to enjoy.

His family and a few of his longtime friends from out of town came to the wedding. I was a great day. I still have people tell me to this day what a great time they had at my wedding. I tell them it was a great day but it was the wrong person. Definitely the wrong person, in fact who did I marry? Well here we go.......

I won our honeymoon! I had gone to a bridal fair and entered my name in a drawing. I won a week's stay on the Big Island of Hawaii. Airfare, condo and rental car all paid for. For real, all paid for. All we did was pay for an upgrade on the car when we got there and that cost us a whole $45. This is where the crap starts to fly off the fan. This fool had no money. Yes, read it again. No money.

He said that he had to help out with the airfare for his grandmother and mother so he sent them the money he had put aside. In my head I'm like what? Luckily I had saved $1,000 and had an entertainment book that helped out with restaurants and some of the tours. We had a great honeymoon and didn't spend all of the $1000 I had brought. I enjoyed the island and have since been back to visit. We talked about it and he apologized for not telling me and promised it would not happen again. He had gotten a promotion and was now with a different State agency. The job was on the other side of town from where we lived. One day he announces that the commute is kicking his butt in gas and he wants a garage for the truck. He feels that we should rent a house. I agree

51

to look at few houses. I also put the word out to several people who live in the general area closer to his job to let me know if any rentals come up in their neighborhood. We look at a few houses and no of them really appeal to us. I figure we would look after Christmas and the New Year. In the meantime, a friend tells me about a house that is going up for rent and will include the refrigerator, washer and dryer. It is a client of hers that is being transferred to the Bay Area and she wants to rent her house out, but is a little leery about putting it on the market and dealing with just anyone that may apply. She tells her about me and I drive by to see the neighborhood. It's in a very nice neighborhood and a newer home. I come home to tell Walter I think I have found us a great deal and he announces that he took money out of the saving account and put it down on one of the houses that we had looked at and needs me to sign the rental agreement. What? He felt the house was fine and it's close to his job and it has the garage we need.

So within five–six weeks this man has shown me he has I issues with money and communication. We move into the house just before Christmas in 1994 and he doesn't want to use his truck. You know the beautiful, gas hog truck that needs a garage. He's lucky enough to find people to help us move and he doesn't want to use his truck other than for light objects and the fish tank. He shows his ass and a friend puts him in check. He apologizes and says it's the stress of moving. Remember the house that I had been told about with the refrigerator, washer and dryer. Well this house had neither. It had a garage for his precious truck. Walter was unable to find a good deal on a used refrigerator (which I knew he wouldn't) so I purchased a new refrigerator on my credit card so that we would at least have food in the house. As far as washing clothes he was told he had to take them to the laundry mat and take care of them, which he did.

After the move and Christmas comes and goes, my mother suggests that we go to Marriage Encounter. She even pays for it. For a weekend in January of 1995, we are at a hotel and the whole focus is to work on your marriage. What marriage? We were married in November and in January we are already at a Marriage Encounter retreat. We had writing exercises to do and talking to do. At one point he went against the whole grain and decided to change the recommitment vows that we had to say to each other. I'm looking at this fool and asking myself "Did the body snatchers come and take Walter away?" Needless to say that was a wasted weekend, a strange encounter and I'm thinking divorce.

A few weeks later he tells me that his son wants to stay with us until he goes into the military which would be 60 days. I told him no problem, we have four bedrooms. As long as he is respectful and cleans up its fine with me. I can get to know him better. I had not spent a lot of time with him and thought it would be a good idea. Walter told me he told him no. I was in shock and a bit pissed. "Why not?" I asked. He states we just got married and we need to work some things out. Besides he can stay with his grandmother. About two months after being in the house (which I hated) he asks me when I am going to put him on my credit cards. I told him "I'm not". He was in shock. "But we're married", he said. "I'm not putting you on my credit cards", I repeated. "I'm trying to get out of debt."

The next thing I knew he brought in some raggedy mattress and box spring and put it in one of the bedrooms and put a tag on the door that he had taken from a hotel that stated "Do Not Disturb". I know you are laughing. I was like no he didn't. I had to chuckle. This boy is having a temper tantrum and he still ain't getting access to my credit cards. Once again, he apologized and stated that he thought we should see a counselor

One day I came home early and found a card addressed to him from a (Quinilla Graham). I wrote down the name and address and thought what a god awful name. I put it on the counter with the rest of the mail. Once again, he apologized and stated that he thought we should see a counselor and he would make the arrangements through the EAP program. He picked the counselor and set the date and time. When I got there he had been there for a while. When we got into the office with the counselor we began to talk. I explained that there were issues with honesty, money and expectations that were causing problems and we needed to talk and get clear on where we were going. I wasn't comfortable with the coldness in the house, the way we moved into the house, his relationship with money and the role he expected me to play.

I remember the question the counselor asked him and his response like it was yesterday. Mr. Butler what is your commitment level with regards to your marriage? His response "I have no commitment, I'm not committing to anything." I shook my head and the counselor looked like she had seen a ghost. After what seemed like a long moment of silence, she asked him "What was the point of setting the appointment, calling and verifying the appointment and then being early for the appointment if there was no commitment?" He just said he wasn't committed to anything. I remember looking at her and stating that our session was over and that I would like to come back for an appointment since we had been approved for 3 sessions. She asked him how was he expecting anyone to help us with our situation if was not committed to anything. She was dumfounded and I was numb.

As we were going down the elevator I was thinking how much longer is the lease on this house and where did I need to start to get myself together to get up out of this relationship. The body snatchers had come and taken the Walter that I had lived with for almost a year and I didn't like let alone love this Walter that I was married to and lived with. Walter went to work as he was working the late shift and came home while I was asleep. Later that day, he called and said that he was going to stay at his friend's house and he would call me tomorrow. Well guess who called that night? You know it was the friend. I told him that he wasn't there and that he was supposed to be staying with him for the night. He told me that he had not talked to him in a few weeks and wasn't going to be a part of his game playing. He stated that he didn't like the changes in him and wasn't sure what was going on but that I deserved better.

The next day he called and stated that he wasn't coming home and would be staying at a truck stop because he needed distance, and time for him to think. I remember thinking you couldn't come up with a better excuse for not coming home. After about an hour I pulled out the address that I had written down and drove over there. It was an apartment complex so I drove around to see if I found his truck and sure enough I did. I called him on his cell phone. No answer. I proceeded to get in the truck and move it across the street in the parking lot.

I came back and called again. No answer. So I then went to the door of her apartment and knocked. She came to the door and I introduced myself and stated that my husband was staying with her. She looked surprised and scared. She stated "We're just friends" and asked me to come in. I went in and stood by the door. She went to another bedroom and knocked on the door and said something to him. He came out and looked like he was sleeping. He was surprised and confused as to why I was there, how did I find him, etc. He stated there's nothing going on. We are just friends. I asked if you are just friends how come I don't know her? I looked around and then told her that "it looks like you just got yourself a roommate". I told him he had one hour to get his sh*t out of the house or else it would be on the front yard and I know he didn't want that because he didn't want anyone knowing his business. I got up and left. He walked out behind me and I was parked where his precious truck was. He threw a fit, jumping up and down shouting, "Where is my truck?" I just laughed to myself, but if looks could kill. I would be dead. I told him to look around and even across the street, he would eventually find it. He found it and before I knew it he was right behind me on my tail looking like he wanted to run me over and kill me. I pulled over and let him pass. I went to the house and within the hour he was there with a friend of his and they were loading his dresser, bed and some of his clothes. I spent the night trying to make sense of the last few months but and I could conclude was that I was his meal ticket and he was through because he did not get his way. That part was true but there was so much more.

The next morning the phone rang at about 7:00 a.m. it was his grandmother. She wanted to talk to him. I told her that he was not there. She asked, what's going on? The last few times I have called he wasn't home. Are ya'll having problems? I stated yes, and then

56

asked if she could possibly shed some light on his recent changes since she had raised him. That is when everything starting falling apart. She said, "What you mean, I ain't raised that boy." I was surprised. Since I have known Walter he has always stated that is grandmother had raised him. I told his grandmother his story and she started to cry. "Everything that boy done told you is a lie", she said. "I haven't raised any of my grandchildren. They come and stay with me during the summer but that's it." "He grew up in Lafayette along with all of his brothers and sister. "You haven't hurt him have you? Cause his first wife tried to stab him with a knife." "He made her awfully mad and she tried to kill him." I said, "No I haven't tried to kill him". I said, "That would be Sherry, right?" She said "No child, Jackie his first wife". What? "I thought he had been married once to Sherry." "No, Sherry is his second wife" she said. What????

She went on to tell me that he and Jackie were married and had a son that she named after him. At some point in time he stated that he found out the boy was not his and they had a heated argument. She tried to stab him and he left. His mother sometimes hears from Jackie, but to her the boy doesn't look like none of them. She then went on to say this to me. "I'm talking to you woman to woman; don't let him get ahold of your money". I found that interesting due to my experience with him asking me to put him on my credit cards. She went on to say that he had gotten out of the military and had gone back to Lafayette. His father and he have the same name and his father had let him use his credit card to buy a nice suit for interviewing. He used the card, charged up $2,500 and decided not to stay in Lafayette. He left town and they didn't know about how much he charged until after he left and they didn't hear from him for about five years. He said "If he does that to his mama and daddy, what he going to do to you?" I was in shock and needed to

57

get myself together. I called into work and decided to go to the court house to see what I could find with regard to the marriages and divorces. Keep in mind this is 1995 and everything was on microfiche.

It took me awhile but I found the information and much more. I discovered that he was married to Jackie in 1977. She finally divorced him in 1993 and had the paperwork sent to his parents' house in Louisiana. He was married to Sherry in 1985 and they divorced in 1990. This makes Walter a bigamist. WOW, a bigamist!! I also found child support filings for his son and daughter. The sons' case showed he had been ordered to pay $50 per month and the daughters' case was not available as it had become active. To make a long story short, he had not paid $50 a month child support for his son and they had begun to garnish his wages once they were able to locate him. The daughters' case was active because his daughters' mother had found out that he had married and wanted more money. The other thing I found interesting was the variations of his names that he used. He went by Walter Butler, W.J. Butler, Willie Charles Butler, Charles Butler, Charles W. Butler and W. Butler Jr. In total there were 11 cases on record for Walter including divorces, paternity and child support. Who the hell did I marry? I asked myself. With all the names I found I started to wonder what his real name was. I came home with copies of the information and put things in order and looked at dates. Later that evening I received a call from his Aunt Mary. I had not met her when I was visiting for Christmas; she was out of town and lived in Houston. She said that she was very confused and her mother (his grandmother) was crying and going on and she couldn't make sense of what she was saying about Walter so she thought she would call. I reiterated the story to her and she stated that everything I told her was a lie. This means that his whole life story was a lie. She said she always thought he was a little weird. She said that everyone was so happy when they met me and thought that he had finally changed and grown up. She heard the wedding was beautiful and everyone was excited for me to come and visit again. We talked for a while and she told me that she wasn't going to tell his mother right away as his father was doing so well and she didn't need the added stress.

Walter had left some boxes at the house and something told me to look through them. I found paperwork regarding yet another child in New Jersey, a cell phone bill for $1,200 with calls to Salinas, CA, and pictures with other women. I put everything back like I found it. In a matter of 72 hours my world had drastically changed but now I was armed with knowledge. You see, I loved and cared about Walter but I was not in love with him. I was done.

I received a call from Walters's mother about a month later. She had learned about our separation. She was shocked, sadden and disappointment in her son. She told me not to feel bad. He had fooled everyone. She had no idea that her son was so messed up. She verified that everything he had told me about his growing up was a lie. I received a nice card and letter from her later in the year expressing how disappointed she was and advising me to hang in and to keep my head high. She stated again for me not to feel bad because he had fooled everyone.

Remember the counselor we had gone to? I went back to the counselor for the last visit and to say that she was shocked and unprepared for my story would be an understatement. This was out of her league and I knew it. I contacted his EAP and made an appointment for myself to talk to someone. I met with a counselor and told her my story. The next visit she had me read a list of characteristics off of a list and asked to make a tally of each one that applied to Walter. Out of 11 of the characteristics listed he met 9 of them based on what I had experienced and had learned about him. The list was in a manual labeled DSM (Diagnostic and Statistical Manual of Mental Disorders). Walter would be diagnosed as a sociopath/pathological Liar.

Sociopaths are very charming and manipulative people. What surprised me was how long he had been able to keep up this front. She and I went over a few events and my assignment was to find the hints that I had missed along the way. My last session would be to go over those.

In the meantime, I received a call at my job from Walter wanting to know if I had taken the truck. In my mind I'm like you are crazy but I was polite and just stated, no. He said that the truck had been stolen and the insurance company wanted him to contact anyone else who had a key. Truth is I had forgotten than I even had a key to his precious truck. He stated I needed to contact the insurance company and let them know. I called and spoke to the adjuster who told me that the truck was outside and the Acura was in the garage. I'm like Acura? I just said that I was surprised the truck wasn't in his garage but that I did have the key and would get it to him.

Wow, I would be willing to bet my yearly salary that is boy had the truck stolen and had a backup car in the garage. I'm sure financed by another woman. It's just too much of a coincidence that the truck was outside and he had another vehicle just waiting for him. You see, I had told him that I wanted my name off of the truck period. Well my name was never taken off of the truck, but the loan was paid off so my credit remained in good standing.

I took the key to him at his job which was on my way to work. He asked how I was doing and stated that he felt bad and wanted to work things out. He then stated "I did everything I was supposed to do to get a woman like you". Did I hear the s sociopath right? Yes I did and this boy just owned up to being a farce. Wow! I mean WOW! This was all calculated and I had been manipulated, lied to, and god only knows what else. I didn't follow along like he had expected and he had just fessed up. He said it like it was a normal thing. Like he didn't have to keep doing what he had been doing in order for things to work out. This is how a sociopath thinks and operates. I just told him I was done and left. We never have had a conversation about what I found out and have proof of. Why would I go to a sociopath/pathological liar and ask him why he lied? He's just going to lie.

I moved out of the house and into an apartment and was moving on with life. He called early in December and stated that we should just move on with the divorce. I stated that I agreed and would deal with it after the first of the year. He wanted to deal with it now. I told him that I was going to enjoy my holiday and would deal with it in January. You see, Walter didn't really care much for Christmas. I told him that I had checked into filing and felt that we didn't need an attorney and that we could file at the courthouse and pay the fees. The only thing I wanted was my maiden name back and my name off of the truck. Since the truck had been stolen and had not been found that wasn't going to be a problem as the debt would be paid off. He wasn't happy but said OK.

On January 5, 1996 I was served with paperwork for a divorce. I fell out laughing. The ladies who delivered the paperwork just looked at me like I was crazy. I asked if they worked for the attorney and they said yes. I laughed and said to them, I hope she gets paid and closed the door. I called the attorneys office a few weeks later and spoke with her. I went to her office and she told me what I needed to file. She stated that he really doesn't need an attorney and I just chuckled. My thought is that it looks good to his next victim that is if he is remotely honest. He can say that he divorced me. I filed my paperwork, paid the fee and the divorce was finalized in August 1996.

Remember my assignment from the counselor was to look back and find out what I had missed. My big red flag was him wanting the truck a week before we got married. My gut said no and I let myself get talked out of it by listening to my coworkers. They ended up being right about the gas. Walter liked the attention he received while in the truck. It was definitely one that you would take a second look at and should have been put is shows. It was not one for just riding around in and it was definitely a gas guzzler.

My second red flag was the lack of relationship with is daughter. She was out of state but I don't recall many conversations with her, cards, gifts or anything that would indicate an ongoing relationship. I found out later that he had told her that he was getting married and that my name was Michelle. That is my middle name.

My biggest mistake was not having a dear friend of mine who was an investigator look him up and see what he could find on him. He had offered and I had not taken him up on his offer. If that had been done I would have never married him. Look at what I found on my own at the courthouse in a few hours. There is no telling what else is out there. For all I know he was a bigamist when we married.

I realized that I was naive and too trusting when it came to relationships. I had never dealt with someone who had what a lot of people would consider a lot of baggage. The reality of life is that at the age of 36, when I got married, the likelihood of finding someone that does not have a child or children and/or has never been married is very slim. I had dated men with children before and they had a relationship with their children and paid child support. The situation with his daughter being out of state was one that I had not dealt with. There were issues with him and the mother but I never was involved and our household was peaceful. I found out after we were married that he had told his daughter my name was Michelle. This was of course after things had begun to unravel so I never addressed why that lie had been told.

His relationship with his son who lived in town didn't seem strange. They talked, hung out and he came by the house. I did not have an opportunity to talk to him by myself but of course during that time I had no questions or suspicions. What was strange was him not wanting his son to live with us, probably because I would have discovered some other lies that had been told. Unfortunately that transpired after we were married. I've learned to go with my gut and investigate. In Sacramento you can now go to www.saccourt.com and look up cases for criminal and family court.

It used to be a free service but now they are charging. I can't tell you how many times I have found out information on men for myself and my friends by using this serve. You don't get all of the details for family issues but you can learn if there are any cases on file for a divorce, paternity and child support. The criminal database gives you dates, charges and outcomes. I found quite a few of my friends have met men that have a record for domestic abuse. I've met men who have lied about being divorced. One even told me that he was divorced in his heart. ☺

A man's relationship with his mother is also important. Walter didn't care for his mother very much. He said he felt she didn't want him because he was raised by his grandmother. Well now knowing the truth and knowing that he didn't care for his mother also sheds light on how he feels about women in general. If a man doesn't have a good relationship with his mother and the children he helped bring into this world I move on. I've also learned to ask questions several times and in different ways to see if the answer is the same. Now Walter was good. His stories were consistent which is what pathological liars are good at. I'm positive he could pass a lie detector test because he believes his story that he has created. But, most people are just not that good. I've also learned that when someone is very charming and knows just what to say, be aware, watch what they do and trust your gut. Walter was just too perfect when we were dating now that I look back. Even when we lived together he was able to keep up a good front. Things didn't start to change until just before the wedding. He seemed to be in a rush. I now view it as him trying to get as much as he could before everything starting catching up with him.

There is a book out called "The Sociopath Next Door". The author estimates that four percent (1 in 25 people) of the population are sociopaths. The book was published in 2006, so that was the estimate at that time. Chances are that you have come across a few sociopaths in your life.

CHAPTER 5

"HIM"

By

Anonymous

Age 34

Antioch, California

You know how you see a guy and think to yourself "damn this niggah is fine!" Imagine having that thought and your sitting in the middle of church service, with your husband in the nearby pew. The truth is I wasn't even thinking about him ever being someone in my life but my mind was just stating the obvious. I mean, I wasn't blind. I do however remember saying to myself, "if I were single and this man approached me, it would be on!" Well I would soon get my opportunity to be faced with that very scenario. I became a widow very abruptly and soon after this same guy I saw in church became very interested in me. I knew I wasn't ready to date, but I couldn't let this chance slip by me without at least giving it a fair shot; mistake number one. When your gut feeling is telling you that you're not ready to entertain something, go with that feeling. I think it was more than that for me though. I was really interested in what he wanted with me. I didn't think I was his type for one, and he had never spoken to me until my husband passed away; nonetheless, I decided to "give this one a shot."

It was Valentine's Day when he first called me (I guess he wanted to be romantic) and although I was busy at school; I agreed to go out with him that evening. Again, this will prove to be a mistake. We were supposed to go to the movies, but instead ended up going out to eat at a place he refused to order food at because he "couldn't find anything on the menu that sounded appetizing." I should have known something was wrong from the beginning because he asked me to meet him in a public parking lot prior to the date, and I ultimately ended up driving. So I'm sitting in this restaurant thinking I'm on a date and he refuses to pay because he "didn't order anything." Mistake number two and three. I met up with him and drove, and I've just paid for our first date. The night gets even better when he asks to use my computer to print and make copies of some divorce papers...his divorce papers. My naïve ass said, "Yes, sure you can use my computer." The truth is I was so attracted to him that I never saw a problem with these series of events. I just continued to entertain this nonsense because I wanted him to see I was "down" and could be a part of his team if he'd let me. Which brings me to mistake number four being too eager too soon trying to impress some superficial bullsh*t.

I knew I was smarter than this, but I didn't want to think that someone I met in the house of the Lord would have any motives against me. I mean he was employed, attractive, religious and getting divorced, how could I go wrong? Our friendship developed very quickly. I found myself becoming more attracted to him, yet more disgusted with him all in the same breath and it was indescribable to say the least. I spent months going back and forth with my better judgment verses my natural feminine urges. Six months after our so called first date, I decided it was time to consummate our (what I thought) relationship. I mean we had been hanging out for months, and he had finalized his divorce. Let's face it, I was getting cold and lonely. I suppose the real truth is I was more interested in satisfying my appetite physically instead of mentally, and I continued to pay for it in self-worth (perhaps I was starting to forget mine). I kept telling myself that the chemistry was there, minus the chauvinistic attitude and resistance to introduce me to anyone in his life; along with the fact that we never did anything other than sit on my couch and watch T.V. I guess we could count the one time he asked me to go to work with him [he was a bus driver], or the two times he asked to go to the movies at the last minute. I have two underage children so last minute things didn't work well. There's also the fact that whenever anyone was about to come over he needed to leave or became paranoid that someone from church may see him hanging out at my home. He had a daughter, but never introduced me yet he knew my kids, ate at my house, and never once invited me over for dinner...or breakfast...not even lunch. Which brings me to mistake number five: giving myself to someone who clearly didn't deserve the pleasure of my company...and the fact that he wasn't open to new ideas, scared to or embarrassed to be seen with me or afraid he'd have to explain himself to someone. All these things should have definitely been a huge red flag but it wasn't. I once again chose to look past all of this because I was "giving him a chance." I know now that I wasn't "giving him a chance," I was just forgetting that I have value, that I have worth, and that I have something special that only someone special should have access to.

Without going into too much detail (mainly because the next few months were stale), the six months we spent getting to know each other wasn't exactly the most pleasant. I'm thinking back to the first time he'd ever come over and proceeded to argue or disagree with me about how I conduct things at my home. I guess that should have been mistake 1 ½. I was now coming to find out that he was controlling, uninterested/involved in my life and interests, rude, cheap (we all got financial issues), boring...did I say

69

controlling? He had nerve to call my Mom one day (got her number from the church directory) to "tell on me" that I had been "mean" to him! Crazy right?? He didn't necessarily give off the vibe that he thought women should think and speak for themselves. Like we should be seen and not heard. Oh did I mention that he had stopped coming to church?...because he had. Religion is very important to me and he was starting to show signs of uncertainty. Again, all signs I neglected to see because I was so mesmerized by looks and societal opinions, thinking "he makes me look good." I didn't like what I was becoming; allowing myself to engage in such low self-esteem behavior and I started to back off of this man. I had begun to feel like I was wasting my time. This was right around Thanksgiving of the same year, now nine months after our first so called date and I decided to take a road trip with the family to Washington State. I had separated myself from him before this trip, and I was under the impression he was more interested in just being my friend (if that was possible now that we've crossed the line). I began the process of once again rearranging my life to being single and not dating for a while.

I was gone for about a week, and even while I was there he was beginning to text me to tell me he missed me. He was wondering when I was coming home, couldn't wait to see me, and saying all the right things a girl wants to hear from someone she's interested in. So long story short I end up home, and by home I mean my mother's house due to the ten hour trip from Washington. No sooner as I walked through the door, my phone was ringing...it was him. This will be mistake number six I believe...not leaving well enough alone. I decided to see him, that same night, because he was finally inviting me over to his house. I thought he was ready to "get his sh*t together"...maybe he was ready to admit he wanted to be more than friends and maybe I should give him another chance. Maybe he was acting off because he was scared to move on. I mean, after all, I was just recuperating from a devastating loss, and he was just getting out of a marriage. I thought maybe our disconnection (outside of the bedroom) was simply due to not being truly ready to jump into a relationship and not ready to admit it. Oh yeah, mistake number seven...just because physical chemistry is great doesn't mean mental chemistry follows. It's like, we both thought the other one was "cool," but that means nothing anymore after nine months of "hanging out;" plus it's not like we're in high school anymore. What the f*ck is "cool?" Are you trying to f*ck with me or not? Two grown ass people should know what they want to do after almost a year.

Back to the night at hand, the evening was nice and I can't say that I had any complaints other than I didn't feel real comfortable at his place; it's like he was being sneaky or something and I felt like more of an intruder than a guest at times. This is now Mistake Number 8...if a man can't make me feel comfortable in his own environment, something is wrong. I am truly embarrassed to say that I continued to entertain this for another month all the way up to Christmas. I actually got this man a gift and was looking forward to seeing him for the holidays. As angry as I was, I was able to get over the fact that he hadn't gotten me a gift (although I know I had deserved one) and we decided to go to the movies (to continue my yearly tradition). I figured this would be his gift. Getting me irritated once again, I was asked by him to drive to the movies which meant I had to pick him up (and in all this year he had only put gas in my car a few times, never full, and he used it several times). Halfway to the movies he starts rambling on about thinking he forgot something at home, or he forgot to do something and I ignored it. We get to the movie counter, ask for the said film, and this motherf*cker pats himself down and says "I forgot my wallet at home." I sh*t you not!! This man actually patted himself down as if he didn't know he didn't have his wallet! That's like a woman leaving her purse at home or some sh*t. Bullsh*t! I was so pissed; too embarrassed to leave the counter, but by this time I was so mad at myself for allowing things to get so far. At that moment I just decided to treat his sorry ass one last time then say "deuces." So you realize this is now Mistake Number 9; allowing someone to make a fool of me and doing nothing to defend myself. I mean, I knew on Valentine's Day we weren't compatible (the first [and only] date), but I kept the bullsh*t going for selfish reasons. Almost a year later, here we are and this fool ain't got $10 for a damn movie. I mean…why'd he even ask me if I wanted to go? Did he really think I was this stupid? Naive? And even though I had been acting pretty dumb, I wasn't.

I had an epiphany that night and I was no longer going to be the doormat for some guy I barely know; who does absolutely nothing to enhance my life. I couldn't believe that I had wasted almost a year entertaining this man, feeding him dinner, letting him spend the night, even the occasional foot rubs. Hell, I even ironed a few shirts for him! I was certain that I would be able to justify why I didn't think we should continue to see each other, but I once again gave in to the idea that we could be "friends" even though he understood that I was no longer interested in having a physical relationship with him. I would still talk to him on the phone maybe once a week or so, and I believe sometime in February the following year (about two months after the Christmas movie incident) he had asked me for a ride to go pick his car up about 50 miles away from my home. I hesitated, but he assured me he would fill up my tank (which he did before we left so we used gas he was supposed to be replacing). He also stated that he wanted to talk. Mistake Number 10: I should have been done with him in

December. On the way we began to discuss the previous year, and what could have possibly went wrong (because we had liked each other) and how could we start over. As crazy as it sounds, I started to believe that maybe we could start over...perhaps we'd put too much pressure on each other the year before. I began to question his motives yet once again. I mean, if this guy didn't genuinely like me, or wasn't interested in me, why was he still hanging around? We hadn't been intimate in months, and let's face it...he had gotten it, so what did he still want? It had to be something about me right?

After a long hard look in the mirror, I decided to just end it by not taking his calls anymore and essentially trying to avoid him at every turn. This tactic worked for a while, but after a few months of this I was starting to believe he wasn't getting the hint. He would leave messages and text me. Although I wouldn't respond, he always seemed to be concerned. My birthday was in June (and no he hadn't gotten me anything the year before) and this year I was throwing myself a house party. Against my better judgment I had invited him, along with a few other men in or around my life. Although he didn't show up, he had dropped off a birthday card to me. It was nothing fancy, but I had appreciated the gesture. Mistake Number 11: based on this invitation he thought I was interested in him still. But, by then I had decided not to be so hard on him and we started to converse again in a very sporadic manner; however, I soon realized that it did little to ease his hurt pride. He just couldn't understand why I didn't want to entertain him anymore. After a few more months of ducking and dodging calls, I felt like I was ready to start the year coming up fresh...no baggage. So the year came to an end with me explaining to him that I'd felt that I had gave him what I thought was ample time to ma.ke sufficient choices about what direction he wanted to go in with me.

I simply felt like I wasn't going to waste any more time. Mistake Number 12: explaining myself to someone who doesn't deserve an explanation because I felt like "I owe him that much." I guess I wanted him to know that he didn't have to prove anything to me anymore (he'd missed his chance), and I realized that we weren't compatible and was okay with that. Because I never told him to stop calling me, he had continued to try to reach out to me for many months following, urging me to reconsider him to be a part of my life even if it's just as a friend. Maybe one day, I'm sure I can find it in my heart to put our nightmare completely out of my mind and be adult enough to be re-introduced to someone I once knew. After all…when I didn't learn anything from Mistake Number 1, I allowed myself to "be the fool" and can now accept full responsibility for my role in this and my actions leading up to a failed attempt at love.

CHAPTER 6

"INTUITION LEADS YOU"

By

Anonymous

Age 33

Bay Area, California

I am a single mother of two in my 30's, with two different men. Not what I ever wanted for myself, I always wanted the princess dream. I wanted the career, house, husband, and kids. I wanted what I did not have growing up. I had my Mom who was and is wonderful but my Father wasn't there. My Father wasn't the best example of what a man was supposed to be. I wanted my kids to have the support of both parents. I wanted them to have someone to depend on besides just me. I wanted my children to know the love of their Father. Something I can honestly say now as a grown woman I never had. I settled on several things I said I never wanted, I settled on relationships that could have been left and never let happened. Growing up, I can remember hearing the older women say listen to your intuition because it will never lead you wrong. Growing up, I wondered what the heck they mean. A woman's intuition is a powerful thing! If more women would just listen to the voice in their hearts, minds and souls; maybe just maybe so many women could avoid the heartache and pain we endure from time to time. Yes, there are things in life that are meant for us to go through, some lessons to be learned and some people to be removed in the way God intended. However, there are those events that intuition warned us before we even got started in, those are not the lesson meant to learn; those are the ones meant to be avoided altogether. Know your worth and listen to your intuition! Here are some questions to ask yourself: Do you know your worth? Do you listen to your intuition? Do you know what you will and will not accept?

One of the first relationship's I ever had was with my oldest child's father. I was about nineteen years old and thought I had met the man of my dreams. The man who was everything I had asked for. I met him through a mutual friend, who swore we were made for one another. Let's call him Ron. I met Ron one evening at his job in Concord, where he worked as a security officer for a big company. At first sight, I just knew I wanted to know more about Ron. You see Ron was a pretty boy, he dressed real nice and always had money. He came from a two parent home, he is the youngest of two. His parents took care of everything for him. Talk about spoiled they bought his car, clothes, and food. He worked just to support his habit of weed and drinking. He lost a few jobs due to this habit. I could remember thinking Ron was the one, we were that lifetime love. We were inseparable, minus us going to work we were always together. Hanging out, parties and all. I started smoking weed when we would hangout. I learned how to drive while high, hell even drunk. This relationship was toxic but when in love you can't see the toxicants. When you are in the relationship you can't see that someone is not good for you. As our relationship progressed, I would become pregnant not once, not twice, but a total of three times by Ron. The first time at twenty years old, making a mutual choice we decided it was best at that time to have an abortion. The abortion would be the start of the change for us. As time went on I realized I didn't really want to have that abortion but did it more so to keep Ron. At this point, once the abortion was done, we would start to argue more and I would really start to smoke and drink every day. I felt as if I was in too deep, it was too late to exit now. I was in too deep because I was pregnant again and I didn't want to be a single mother at all. I would settle for a drug head and alcoholic. I would decide to keep this child, this is our love child so I thought. We are meant to be, I'm pregnant again. During this pregnancy is when red flags started to appear. Red flag, I had never met his parents and at this point we have been together for about a year and a half. Red flag, I am five months pregnant, his parents don't even know about our unborn child. As time passed I would take a roller coaster ride of a lifetime. As my pregnancy progressed, I would realize Ron wasn't just smoking weed but it was laced with something called "white girl" (cocaine). He would become distant and start cheating. He would have me take him to another girl's house, unknowingly. So much would happen over the course of a few months. You see I would carry this child for five months, at which time I will find out at an appointment not only does this child have a rare lung defect; this pregnancy would end differently. His parents still would not know of my son till the day he was born to die.

At twenty weeks pregnant, I would find out at my ultrasound that my baby was not growing correctly. We went to the doctor together, to be told to leave from the office and go right to the hospital; our son would be born today and died shortly after birth. As we left the doctor's office he would call his mom to tell her and of course her being in shock, everything truly started to go downhill. I would be called all kinds of names, be told how they would have never picked me to be with their son, and how I should just let the State throw my baby away. Nicely put Ron's parents did not like me at all! Ron and I would continue to date for roughly one more year, when I'd become pregnant yet again with our third and final child together. Throughout this pregnancy Ron was homeless, jobless, and mean. But I held on because we were having yet another child. I held on because I didn't want to be single and I felt I couldn't get anyone better. However, Ron and God had a different plan for me. Three days after I gave birth to my last child, Ron would walk due to his parents not liking me. The next few years I would go through all kinds of emotions and life changes. I would reject my child because Ron had rejected me. Looking back I can honestly see where I let go of our child because he had walked out on me. What I was taught from Ron is because I had problems within myself, I held on to someone who didn't value me. I kept dealing with the disrespect, distrust and dishonesty. Several times throughout my relationship with Ron, yet something kept saying get out. When we would take "breaks" I would always hear that voice say now is your chance for a clean break.

Sadly history would repeat itself when I met my second child's father. Although it would be sometime before I realized it and that it would be present in a different form. By the time I met Jarvis I had been single for about two years. I had just been enjoying life. Jarvis and I met on one of those dating site, he reached out to me. First voice said don't even start this relationship, he is too young. You see Jarvis is seven years younger than myself. It started different, I seen it as let's just have fun. I never planned on falling for him or going any deeper than a few drinks, a party or two and end it. The next three years would be a worst roller coaster ride than the last. When it came to Jarvis I lost myself and I became a whole different person. Since at this point I didn't have a relationship with my oldest daughter, it was easy to just leave her. It was easy to create a relationship with a young guy that wanted to be on the go. That lasted for so long, see he started not wanting me to go with him or meet up with him or be around. Red flags, yet again but different because I met his family right away within

78

about two weeks. Family BBQ's, outings, and just hanging out at the house with them. Jarvis had me fooled, like I knew everything about everyone we were around. Oh, the lies! When all was said and done with Jarvis and me, he had a total of three kids under five years old by two different women. Over the course of our relationship we went through a lot. I lost myself behind him and did things that changed me. I have always been a helper and Jarvis played on that. If he needed I gave, if he wanted I made a way of getting it for him; and if he said to do, I did. Jarvis played on my core. When we met I told him what I wanted and what I was looking to have in life. He made me believe that is where he was headed. A year and a half into it, things slowly took a turn. The compliments stopped, the always wanting me around stopped and the him helping me stopped. The whole relationship turned into myself helping him at any cost. For almost a year, I rented out cars for Jarvis sometimes he paid but for the most I did. When we would take trips I'd be the one paying. Every time I would do something I would hear that little voice saying not to do or to think first before I did it. He had sold me on a dream that I wanted for so long it was hard to listen to that little voice inside. He sold me on the family, always around his family, his mom being super friendly and me meeting everyone. I worked at a big company and I ended up losing my job because I was unable to tell this guy no and mean it. I helped his family in any way I could. However, when I look back I was used by all parties. Jarvis cheated not once, not twice but multiple times. Every time he got caught he had a different story, each one better than the last. At two years in, I was pregnant for the second time by him and this time I'd keep my baby. Six months into my pregnancy with our child I found out he had another one the way. In his words "he slept with her because he was mad at me. He was mad I was pregnant and keeping it. That put a monkey wrench in his plans." Not sure how that was true. Within six months of each other myself and the other female had babies. Mine being the oldest. Six months after that she was pregnant again. That's when I decided to leave. That is when I could really hear that voice telling me it was not going anywhere that I expected. If a person shows you who they are over and over again, they are not lying. Trust they are presenting their true self, and if it looks shady they probably are just that.

See if you just listen to the voice inside it will guide you. Granted if I didn't go through things with Ron and Jarvis, I wouldn't be who I am today. Yet I could have avoided a lot of the pain I went through had I left when the chances were presented. Women will stay in an unhealthy situation just to have someone, to not be alone or to feel needed. We will ignore that voice sometimes at all costs. We will lose relationships with people that mean the most to us, like our children, parents, family, and friends. Sometime we will lie, cheat and steal for these men. Taking the consequences such as jail, house arrest, and parole. We will become someone we do not recognize in the mirror to have him stay. You see we have that intuition, that voice inside us to help us, to keep us on track. We have that voice to allow us to be great and not succumb to a man. Women are powerful if only we used our mind, intuition, and courage. A lot of the pain, heartbreak, and misleading stuff we endure would be avoided.

Think about it what is most important to you? What are your values? At the start of your relationship with a man, think about writing a list of each of your top five most important values. Weigh your values against one another. Once you do this you should know if it is worth going further or not. Once you know your values, you know what you will and will not put up with. You will no longer take dates just to get out the house, being alone will not matter, and you will use your values to better your life. You will no longer be looking for love, you will no longer be in search of that perfect family, and you will no longer be holding on to that dream. You will work on you and your values. You see that inner voice also known as woman's intuition is not some pawn but it is your values trying to keep you focused on them. It is that mother, grandmother, sister, aunt and friend saying they remember you are better than that or this. Your values are deeper and should deliver better if you just stick to them. That inner voice is your memories past of where you have come from, what you went through, and where you are headed. Think of your inner voice/woman's intuition as a personal alarm when you are being robbed at gunpoint for your values. When you are being taken for the ride of your life.

I have lived through that ride, that robbery and that gunpoint. I have been sent through the ringer and back for my values. So by choice the last two years I have been single. I have been working on me as a woman, mother, daughter, and friend. I am rebuilding my life currently serving a year house arrest sentence. Rebuilding relationships with my family and children while rebuilding a career. My past relationships created hurt, pain, and for me losing my values. I have always been a friendly, trusting, easy going, and light hearted person. I have always told the truth no matter how much trouble I got in. However, after my past relationships I trust no man, I felt I was a liar and I had shamed myself. Now I question every word, action, and gesture presented to me. I listen to the inner voice way more than ever. One thing about that voice it always brings me back to my values. If I had I done this before I could have more than likely held on to my core values. Perhaps had I done that before maybe I would not have went through so much. If I held on to my values back then maybe now I could look at myself in the mirror. I lost me, I lost who I was and what I was about to please someone else. I now know my values not that I ever forgot them. I just had to remember where I stored them. I know what I was taught and I now truly know what I will and will not accept. I know my worth now. I pray that God guides and leads my steps. I concentrate on being a mother and showing my girls what they want and don't; what they will and won't accept. Relearning me, loving me, respecting me, and honoring me. If you never learn how to value the real you, you can never expect a man to value you. God first, family, and career those are values.

CHAPTER 7

"SINGLE FOR A REASON"

By

Cheneqa P. Rivers, Age 39

Sacramento, California

After being in a committed relationship for over a year and a half with a man I was planning to marry, everything came crumbling down around me when I was made aware by his mistress that he had been cheating on me for who knows how long with her. Granted there were traces of him lying, sneaking around, and not being accountable for his time; however, I chose to overlook them. But it was with the first substantial lie that he wasn't even single when we met each other and he was actually at the end of his current relationship that I figured his lying was minuscule to me in the grand scheme of things at the time because we had already been dating for over six months. I wish I would have walked away then.

Even though I knew that this other person existed in his life, I chose to stay because at that point I felt like I loved him and I knew that he loved me. I recognized that I should have walked away but I told him that he had to choose between me and her. Hence with his words and some actions he chose me. Within that six month period we spoke regularly for hours over the phone and in person about our core values, our understanding of the bible, our love for our families, and our love for one another. We had developed a friendship that I had been missing in my life. We spent as much time as possible together even though he lived 30 minutes from me in another city. It was against my better judgment, but I pursued this relationship that was developing between us.

After about eight to nine months into our relationship, I met his family including his siblings, his mother, and two children from a previous marriage. Everyone seemed really nice and we all got along pretty well. It was such a great thing to see that his kids got along with my son as well. About a month later he revealed he had another child aside from the two that I already knew about. Come to find out the only reason he told me about this child he had back when he was in high school is that his son had to come to live with him. I accepted the child and the lie that he had committed by way of omission.

It was with this new change in his life that we decided that he and his oldest child should relocate to my city and live with me and my son. We came to the agreement that he would commute for the month of school that was left. When the summer started the kids would be able to stay home together and he would look for work in my city. Within 2 ½ weeks he began to complain about the daily 30-45 minutes one way commute and decided that it would be better for him to move back to his home town at least until school was out. I agreed and with him even though I didn't want them to leave but it was more important to me to keep the peace between him and me than it was to press my point of view. By this time we are a year and few months in and he has now proposed to me and has developed a relationship with my son and my parents. Even though I had some reservations about what he was doing while we were apart and I was 30 minutes away from him, I still trusted him to be faithful to me and our new engagement.

It was the weekend of Father's day and after we had spent time together ALL weekend. I got to work Monday morning feeling happy and overjoyed at the weekend's events. I sat down and began my work day as normal. As I was checking my emails I came across one from a telephone number I didn't recognize with the Subject Line: "Check This Out". It was from his mistress! She had hacked into his laptop and emailed me a photo of him NAKED in his home from her phone. I took a small breath and tried my best not to cry. As I sat at my desk with the daily goings on of my office happening around me, I became conscious of the fact that this was the straw that broke the camel's back!

I immediately contacted him and asked him a series of questions about his whereabouts the night before and where he was and who he was with after I had left to come back home. He couldn't come up with a valid answer so I told him we needed to talk when I got off work that day. I drove out to his home and we went to a local park and spoke about the whole situation. I told him that I loved him enough to forgive him and move on, but I would never tolerate this happening again in LIFE! He promised me that it would never happen again because he made a mistake and loved me too much to lose me. He stated that he couldn't imagine his life without me and that I was the best thing that happened to him!

In spite of the cheating on his part, we tried to push past it because we both loved each other and still wanted to make our relationship work. Things went back to normal between us. We still did things as family and always enjoyed our time together but after a few months it became painfully evident that he was unable to be in a committed relationship with anyone. After some missed calls, cancelled dates, and unanswered text messages, I began to "investigate". There were multiple text messages and voice mails that solidified the fact that not only was he cheating on me with his ex-girlfriend; he had as well acquired a few other women along the way.

As a consequence of his actions, we mutually agreed to end our relationship. We kept in touch for a few months after all these things happened but it was so painful for me to even hear his voice. I eventually severed all ties with him and his family. I understood the things that had happened couldn't be reversed from either of our memories. The pain that I felt was so deep that it was going to take a significant amount of time to heal from this whole ordeal.

After it was all said and done that relationship changed my outlook on what I believed relationships should be and what it took to build solid ones with the opposite sex. I had to realize that a man will tell a woman whatever they think she wants to hear to keep her in their lives. I had to open my mind to actually LISTEN to what was being said to me by a man that I was interested in and not just allow myself to be so caught up by what I saw before me.

It was with that understanding I began to observe men differently and I began to use my mind to listen, see, and value or devalue what was being said to me. I also made a commitment to myself to work on being the women I was intended to be, whether I stayed single or entered into a committed relationship. During the process of healing from my heart being broken, a lot of "growing up" took place within me and I was able to rebuild myself with the help of a lot of praying and spending time with myself. In that time, which was at least two years, I became a stronger and wiser woman. I began to understand and practice the single life. I have continued to be single since that relationship because now I recognize the value of myself and the importance of loving myself enough NOT to devalue my worth by starting, cultivating, or staying in a romantic relationship with a person who isn't ready to be fully committed to me.

I developed a few ideas that I have held onto and those are:

- Some folks are unwilling to give what it takes for my worth.

- I am not afraid to be single until God sends me to a man that is prepared to be the husband intended for me. It is said in the Word that; "The man who finds a wife finds a treasure, and he receives favor from the Lord." Proverbs 18:22; and

- Most of all there is no need to rush into a relationship that is meant to last forever, so I know now that I am single for a reason.

Chapter 8

"How Do You Know When To Get Out?"

By

Anonymous

Age 75+

Bay Area, California

To tell you about my life in relationships, I may have to set the era for you. I was a teenager in the late 40's/early 50's so things were very different especially when it came to dating. Back then I don't think that we thought of any warning signs especially being a young bride. Majority of women got married in their teen years. I am not sure if I wanted to get married but I was pregnant with my first child. I got pregnant the first time I had sex. We got married and had our first child by age 16 and within 13 months, I had my second child. After our second child, I learned he fathered another child with another woman who named her daughter the same name as my daughter. The fighting started after our first child and it only got worse by the week. My parents would have issues in their relationship sometimes, so I think I felt some things were normal. I am not even sure why I accepted this because is not okay to have an outside child especially being already married. The first real issue we had was his infidelity but within the next year, we were having our third child. Before our third child was born, I had left him due to the physical abuse. Sometimes, I would leave at 2:00 a.m. or 3:00 a.m. in the morning but he would call my mother's pleading and saying he loved me and I would go right back. I remember being hit so hard that I was thrown down to the ground.

After going back within a year and a half we had our fourth child. I thought I was in love but I didn't think the abuse was love. My mother would tell my husband, "If you don't know how to treat her, bring her back where you got her from." I would always return to my parents during the times I left him. I would even leave walking late at night with all my small children and one on my hip, just so I could get away. It seemed like the abuse would never stop. He had even abused me while I was pregnant and I called the police but they did nothing. Back in the 1950's domestic violence was not viewed as serious as it is now especially with married couples. I am not sure if I truly had much choice about staying with him especially having all the children and needing to be able to provide for them. I worked picking walnuts and at the cannery which wasn't much pay but it wasn't enough to provide for all my children alone. One thing, I did was work but I remember having to leave work one time because I was so sore from a beating. The abuse affected my life in many areas so when I think back, I am not sure why I kept going back.

After our fifth child, I tried many times to obtain some birth control or have my tubes tied; however, they told me I was too young. After this, I guess I thought I would just have all the children God allowed me too. However, if it were not for the children I am sure I wouldn't have stayed with him as long. I later began cheating simply because he would, and I would think this must be what people do. I thought it was the thing to do not knowing any better due to still being so young.

After we officially split up, I applied for assistance and it was tough back then. I was made to feel so ashamed and put down by the social worker who interviewed me. The worker even asked questions like "when was the last time I had sex," and I was so embarrassed even though I was married. After the interview I was told that I wasn't even eligible for cash aid for three months even though I had five kids. I would only be given vouchers for rent, PG&E, water, and garbage bill. We couldn't even buy any household items. At this point, I was pregnant with our sixth child and I knew that welfare was not for me. I only got $60.00 child support. I had to use the $60.00 to buy all my kids school clothes. I had to report the $60.00 to welfare and the worker told me that I was not supposed to spend the $60.00 and that I needed to give it to welfare. I walked two miles with my five kids to bring her the change from the $60.00 as ordered. Welfare made me feel as if it was a punishment to receive help and I felt that they wanted me to go back to the abusive situation. I knew from then on that I couldn't be a welfare mom, and at that moment I realized that the welfare was not set up to help battered women at all.

I left after that last beating, he drug me around the house by my hair; moreover, this time he wasn't so lucky because he went to jail. There were times he hit me so hard that I saw stars. He got released within two days and I had packed his clothes so he could leave. Before this last beating, I told the Lord that if he hit me again, I would leave forever. After he drug me around the house that last time, I thought he was going to kill me. After he was released, of course he came back apologizing but to no avail. After I informed him that we were not living together anymore, he told me that I was lucky that he had time to think on the ride home from jail. He said that, I was lucky he had time to think because he would have killed me if he got released in the same city. Times were already hard especially financially. I had 5 kids with one on the way and I had left him for good while being pregnant with my sixth child. We had no food or electricity in the house. Most times, we ate one meal a day and I wouldn't tell anyone we were living this way because I was so ashamed. I had to realize couldn't be ashamed or prideful because pride doesn't do nothing for you. I had to realize pride would do nothing for me or my children. I didn't care how much money I made, I had to work. After time passed, I felt better and finally started to feel like I mattered. I really missed him but not enough to be abused any longer. I was truly afraid for my life if I stayed especially after six kids and eight years. I almost had a child every year and I don't know how I made it.

They say that only you know when you have truly had enough in a toxic relationship. At that point, I placed my full trust in the Lord and I knew I would never allow a man to abuse me. It took time after leaving him to understand that life was worth living. Most of the time, I think its best to fully remove yourself from the situation to gain any true clarity. I made a promise to the Lord that if he ever put his hands on me after this, I would never go back. I kept my promise as hard as it was. I was truly afraid he would kill me. After he fought me, he would force me to have sex with him; furthermore, the abuse was not only physical, it was sexual. I didn't even know how to heal from the sexual abuse. I think he felt it was his right to do this no matter how I felt.

When my last son (6ᵗʰ child) was an infant; I went to my neighbor's house and met a man named Avery. He invited me out to eat and to come out on the base with him because he was in the Army. We started dating and oddly neither he nor I even thought about the fact that I had six children. It's hard to say how I truly how felt having this good man in my life after being put through so much abuse from my ex-husband. I do remember it was a long time before I was able to speak upon my ex without tears rolling down my face. I now had this awesome man in this life. The relationship was great and healthy unlike my past relationship but I knew that I didn't want to live with another man without being married. Things were not perfect but nowhere near like my last marriage. He would even take my six children down to the street to see their father; even though it made me upset because I had never stopped my ex from seeing his children; however, it showed me that he was a nice man to make sure the children saw their father. I became pregnant with my seventh child (our 1st child together) and I still could not get birth control pills. Avery and I had spoken about marriage but after my divorce was final, I asked him what are we going to do?

We decided we would not continue to live together being unmarried. Like the old saying goes, why pay for the milk when you could get the cow free; meaning that I could not continue to give myself to any man without marriage, love, and respect. I say this also because when you look in the bible it says, God wants man and woman to marry. I feel many women are willing to give some of themselves including their bodies; without being a man being fully committed. Avery was a great man and an amazing provider especially for my children. This was a love I never knew because all I knew was abuse before him. We went to Reno and got married. We had a good life together and we stayed married for over 40 years until his passing.

After having years to think about everything I can say that if I had to say what my first mistake was is getting married simply because I was pregnant. I felt that none of that would have happened if I would have waited to have sex. I felt by me having sex at such a young age and us being so young and immature, it may have played a huge part in not using my better judgment. We never thought about birth control or anything from our lack of experience being so young. This is why now; I firmly believe that it is extremely important to educate your children.

When I think back I really didn't have anyone to encourage me or instill goals in me. Sometimes I felt like since I had so many kids, life was hopeless. There was this truant officer at our school, his name was Mr. Amquest. Mr. Amquest would stop by my house and encourage me to go to school and get my high school diploma. After having seven kids, I graduated with a GED and high school diploma; despite, the social worker telling me that I didn't need to attend school since I had seven kids. After all I had been through; I had to thank God because he was the only one who brought me through that. I had been through so much, I had never thought I would go onto accomplish everything I have in my life. Even having seven kids, I always worked but God is the true reason I was brought from darkness to light. I worked from picking in the fields to eventually going to college. I actually felt I got in college by accident because I was only taking an acquaintance to college to take a test. I went to take her to take the test and as I sat there, I thought to myself, I may as well take the test too. I took the test and she failed but I passed. After I discovered I passed, I had never really thought about what I truly wanted to do in life. I started taking nursing classes even though I had seven kids under the age of 13. I would think back to my first husband and realize that I was so consumed with the abuse and having children that I didn't think about my future. At times it seemed I lost myself being so consumed in an unhealthy relationship. I also didn't even have time to make friend nor did I have anyone to truly talk to. I really didn't have friends but I had a college professor took a liking to me.

My professor saw something in me that I didn't see in myself even though I almost failed her class. I ended up taking the State board test for nursing and I had one of the highest scores.

I learned that the Lord can bring you through ANYTHING PERIOD. God had placed people in my life who showed me that after all I been through that I was worthy of love. Women can make the mistakes of allowing a man to make them feel as though they are not worthy of love but we must remember God made us to be loved. It took my college professors and the support of my husband to show me I was worthy of love. I remember being a model and my husband would be sitting in the front row smiling and encouraging me. I think one can get so invested in a relationship especially being such a young mother that you can lose your childhood. I felt I never had time to be a child which eventually affected me mentally as well as affecting my relationships and my children.

I want to end this chapter with this message:

If I could send a message to young women these days, I would say stay in school and get an education no matter what. Do not let a bad relationship be your whole life that you don't see much outside of that. Try to take advantage of life before you have children. The older folks used to say, "Take time to smell the roses". I think these days many women make the mistake of moving too fast and not allowing time to get to know someone before jumping in a relationship.

Never let a relationship define you. God will work and prayer works. God knows what you need and don't need. He doesn't' promise to supply your wants but he promises to supply your needs. If I could go through what I went through and accomplished having seven children, you can do anything. When it comes to red flags, I think I may have been too young to know what the signs were. After being through so much, I can tell you this is what I learned: We as women must know what we want in a man and that doesn't include allowing anyone to emotionally, verbally, or physically abuse you. Abuse is abuse period, doesn't matter if it's a push or a punch. Abusive relationships don't just hurt you; they hurt your children too. Many people can tell you that they wouldn't put up with abuse but it's easy to say this until it happens to you. It's also easy for others to tell you to simply leave the relationship. You know from your intuition when something is not right for you and abuse is never okay! Abuse will never equal love. There are no "Big I's and little You's" in a marriage. In relationships, it's not who makes the most money; it's the love, respect, and communication.

My parents would tell me pray and give it to God but I never understood what they meant until I started to get on my knees to pray; however, after praying I would get back up with the same problems. Many women these days are so independent that they want to solve the problem in the relationship themselves but it can make it worse. I realized that even though I was praying, I wasn't truly giving it to God. God wants us to fully trust him yet we want to do it ourselves. You can give the problem to God but your actions must follow. I think the problem with some people is not knowing when to let a relationship go like knowing when its time to give it to God and walk away. Put your full trust and faith in God and let him lead you, for God will never steer you wrong.

Be sure to educate your children about sex, domestic violence, and self-worth.

CHAPTER 9

"NO ONE TO TRUST"

By

AMANDA "DoSSa" DOSS

Age 36

Antioch, CA

STOP – Hold on! You know that feeling you get when you KNOW something just does not feel right or you have a burning question that you are reluctant to ask the person you are with? Well, that Honey Boom (yes I went waaaay back with it) could be the unexplainable intuition that is given to all humans. I won't generalize and say only women, because I believe we all are blessed the same spiritually by a higher power, we just have to tap into those blessings. I have had a many burning questions and ignored feelings that will relate to virtually any girl or woman. Some questions were never answered and ignored feelings gone unaddressed. Now I choose to listen more often and be grateful for whatever comes from it and pay attention to the red flags!

"According to the Partnership Against Domestic Violence, every nine seconds, another woman in the U.S. is beaten." [1] It's a sobering reality for one in four women in our country who will experience domestic violence in her lifetime, most of these victims between the ages of 20 and 24, according to the nonprofit Safe Horizon[2]. Violence against women may occur mostly behind closed doors—60 percent of domestic violence happens at home—but that doesn't mean the problem is any less visible. It pours out into the streets—domestic violence is the third leading cause of homelessness among families—and into future generations. Girls who witness domestic violence and don't receive help are more likely to enter an abusive relationship as a teen. And boys from families of domestic violence are far more likely to become abusers as teens and adults, if no one intervenes." [4]

I wouldn't say growing up in Oakland was hard, but I would say that is was surprisingly more comfortable than finishing my last two years of high school in what they would call "the suburbs". My parents wanted a "better" life for us, as the activities that I was indulging in, were not in line with graduating from high school in a timely manner or at all. My first day of high school for my junior year was scary; a complete culture shock as I had never been around so many Caucasian people in my entire life (16 years of age). The feeling of not knowing anyone and being accepted all seem to pull up some old questions related to fear like, what will people think of me and can they see my fear. Operation hard exterior was immediately put in place. At least until I met someone that I could sort of let my guard down with, but never all the way.

I was about eight when it happened – maybe even ten. I was old enough to know that what took place wasn't right. I was aware enough to know that I wasn't dreaming and it was a reality. I was brave enough to speak the truth in that moment. I believe it was the strength of my older sister that allowed for the truth to be told that night. He was a close friend of our father; a person we would call uncle and on one of the many nights my parents would have parties at the house, he (the uncle) decided to make a pretend visit to the restroom and detour to me and my sister's room. It took some time before my sister and I discussed the details of what we remembered to have happened, but I can see the picture in my head of his hand reaching over the top of the bunk bed to fondle me in a place that a girl at my age should not have known was an attractive area for a man.

I recall slapping his hand away from me as his touch woke me up from my sleep. I heard a loud thump as he exited the room and I called down to my sister. I don't recall all that was said, but we made our way out of the room and into the living/dining room to tell our parents what had happened. The man we knew as uncle was sitting at the table with my parents as if nothing took place. Somehow the conversation and altercation was taken outside between him and our father and we never seen him again in our home. This was the first of three inappropriate incidents that occurred in my childhood. From the baby sitter (female) to a family member – as a child – trust was broken, however, I knew that my parents were not at fault and they did their best with what tools they had. I briefly recall therapy sessions with my parents and my sister, but I did not retain any of what was said or the outcome. But I know that these incidents stayed with me in the back of my conscience throughout my teenage years and now adulthood, which led to my actions and decisions from brokenness. Some people would say I had the makings of a rough childhood from where I came from to the situations that occurred, but I say my childhood is what has molded me to make me see that you can survive pain, fear, heartache, confusion and still live a life of purpose.

From a young lady to a grown woman, every relationship I had, whether it was a friendship or intimate one with a man, was a red flag. Not only did I trust no one, I was always secretly thinking everyone was out to take advantage of me. Without the understanding and forgiveness that I needed regarding what had happened to me, the distrust, pain and fear carried on with me into relationships with boys and later men. At the age of 15, I seen, heard, been a part of and initiated things that were contrary to anything I would like for my daughter to see, think or do. I had a boyfriend that was 5 years my senior at the age of 15 and at the time I was not thinking about what we had in common, but rather thinking *"OH he cute and he have a nice car!"* So I proceeded into this relationship and not with ANY form of caution. This is where I learned about domestic violence and mental abuse in a relationship, not even realizing the sexual abuse in it. In my mind at the time, it was no surprise that a man of an older age wanted me sexually; however, I had not been exposed to the physical abuse from a man to a woman. I had felt like his explosions were my fault and that my words triggered his behavior not understanding that everyone has a choice when they know better. I recall telling my Dad part of the story but not all, fearing that he would never allow me to see him again if that is what I chose to do. Not trusting that my father would have my best interest at heart. I was the example of a child, trying to be an adult and make my own life changing decisions.

The first altercation was at a dinner for my sister's birthday. The boyfriend five years my senior at the time got upset with me about something I had said about him leaving if he didn't want to be there. (Sarcasm runs ramped in my family, however, ladies and gentlemen that is no excuse for someone to verbally abuse or physically assault you). He proceeded to yell at me and ask "Why do you always have to act like a B*tch when we go out." My response was for him to leave since it was a dinner for my sister. He proceeded to get up out of his chair, throw the hardback restaurant menu at my head, chase me around the table, kick the chair and then storm out of the restaurant. Once dinner commenced, he was waiting in the parking lot, ready to apologize. I knew then, this was wrong, I knew that I didn't deserve to be spoken to in that way or assaulted in that way. I was a child. A 15 year old child. This incident, I did tell my father about and I ended the relationship. Later, the boyfriend five years my senior said "He just wasn't ready for me". Until this day, I don't know what that even means but the bruises of that experience remained. I had what I felt like were many friends in high school and moving from Oakland California to the suburbs, may have been a huge culture shock back in 1995. Change was good in a sense that the move gave me a different focus on life and I wanted to graduate. I hadn't thought about my past for years and I was in denial about it pretty much being behind me, never connecting the dots to how I was dealing with boys at the time. Well, it happened at 18, I was hanging around a person I thought was a friend and we drove in my car to another city to visit an older man she was seeing. By older, I mean we were 18 and he was in his 30's, maybe even older now that I reflect back. This was a huge RED FLAG that I ignored because I was NOT at all comfortable with being around older men. I should not have been hanging out with her and I knew it then however, I didn't want her to see me as a disloyal friend and I was still lost, not trusting myself or the Creator. Over that weekend, I remember hanging out and drinking. The one night my friend over drank and passed out, her man friend decided to take advantage of what he thought was a good opportunity with me on the couch. I had drunk way too much and was out of it. I was laying down facing inward to the couch with my back facing outward and felt this heavy pressure against my body. I felt his hand lift up my dress and although I was drunk I was still coherent enough to say No and stop and other choice words. 190 pound man compared to 110 pound girl, I was outweighed and my friend was of no assistance passed out in the next room. "What is he doing, if I struggle, will he hit me?" Did I invite this, did my friend tell him to come out to me, how well do I really know her," were all questions going through my mind as I was crying and saying No, stop and moving around as much as I could. I was outdone and didn't understand why in my life, people just wanted to take advantage of me in a sexual way. After he was done, I just laid there thinking, I can't just leave her here, what if he does the same to her. So I waited on her to get up the next morning so we could leave and it seemed like she took forever. Shockingly, he was up before her and actually asked me to go to breakfast and that we could bring her back some food. I was all confused and didn't know how to react so I went. While at breakfast he made reference to what had happened last night in a way like it was consensual and my stomach just turned. He attempted to grab my foot underneath the table to place it on his private part. I immediately pulled it back. When we got back to the apartment, she was awake and I was eager to leave. I remember not telling her what had happened initially because I didn't know how she would react, and I didn't know if I could trust her. Once I dropped her off to where she was staying, we didn't speak for a while and I had later learned that he told her that I was the one who consented and wanted it. Some would say, I should have done XYZ or question my actions, but you never know what you would do until it happens to you. Our friendship did not continue pass that day. So outside of her, I have remained silent until now only speaking on this situation with someone I was sure not to later use it against me.

Love was still good with someone I had known since I was 14. We were careless and bore a daughter out of that love but our three year relationship overall was full of immaturity, distrust and verbal abuse at times. When someone calls you a b*tch and threaten to kill you out of anger – you need put your cross country shoes on and R.U.N. (Realize Upon Notice) and not look back. I wasn't seeing any red flags because I had not yet grown the stick that would hold the flag to be seen! By the stick; I mean awareness. Even with all that has transpired from the age of 10 until 18, I was still very much without guidance for relationships, understanding of my past, and courage to withdraw at the first sign of unhealthy behavior and security.

He was the one I wrote in my diary about. He was the one I proclaimed as my baby daddy and you know what? That's EXACTLY what I got; A Baby Daddy! Not a father for my child, a husband, someone I can trust, depend on, support, love or encourage. I wrote that proclamation at 14 and it came true at 18. Be careful of what you write into fruition. Writing is powerful and from this experience I have learned to write my plans of greatness down and not my minor altercations, hurt feelings or negative thoughts. Being a teen with hormonal changes was difficult enough and being a teen mom was that much more difficult. My mom says when I had my daughter – she saw me looking at her (my daughter) with a look of "what am I going to do with her". I was 19 years of age, my sister had already had a child at an early age as well and I had NO idea what to do or how to feel. They normally call this postpartum depression – but I could have sworn Life as I knew it – was OVER! No more dancing, partying, singing, hanging out, NOTHING! Dancing and singing was a huge part of my life, although it did not completely cease, I did feel like me pursuing it

105

as a career was impossible due to me having a daughter; I was wrong.

I was raised to believe that a man should be a provider and protector. I didn't understand how a man could ask a woman for money or not have his portion of rent or living expenses. I was 20 when we moved in together. I was hell bent on getting out of my parents' house and being on my own. So I moved fast unnecessarily which put a bigger strain on our relationship as already immature young adults with a life to care for. I was ready, so I thought and he was not. The first sign of difficulty or confirmation that I couldn't trust anyone was when the agreement was broken because he did not have his part of the rent. I was furious as I was working FULL time; paying child care and here you are and can't at least meet me halfway! Not to mention prior, there was incidents of finding phone numbers in the pockets and hearing about random acts of disrespect when he wasn't in my presence. I will admit – there was NO understanding on my part! I couldn't even fathom it, cause my Dad was a provider and that is what I had been used too. This upset me more than being cheated on. I didn't pay attention to the upbringing of this person. The relationship he had with his Dad and lack thereof with his Mom. I didn't know to even pay attention to that. In a lot of ways, I navigated through this relationship with a blindfold. I was still learning to be a mother, caretaker, provider, worker of the corporate world and then partner to someone I felt like wasn't living up to being a MAN. The Man my father showed should be. Knowing I felt this way – eventually led to the demise of the relationship and I was looking for any reason to end it. So as soon as I felt disrespected in ANY way, I changed the locks and left his clothing on the porch with the blender, (ALL that he had brought into the apartment, anyway). It may not have been the best way to handle it, but I used the tools I had at the time, which was very few. This only led to a cycle of domestic altercations and continuous court battles about child support because the resentment was so built up and no one was trying to resolve it for our child's best interest. From this I learned patience is needed, every man is not like my father and to pay attention to what people show you more than what they say.

For a long seven years I was in and out of a repeated cycle of attracting the men that are complete opposite of my father; Cheaters, Liars, Momma's boys and inabilities to be that provider and protector that I needed. I even entertained a noncommittal situation off and on for five years knowing that eventually I would want more and not be satisfied with how things were. Now don't get me wrong, I did NOT want to commit to every man I dealt with. I was very capable of not having ANY emotional attachment or intimacy with people I have dealt with. But it was the couple of men that had managed to make me feel emotionally and physically safe that I latched on to the most and the first sign that my safety was in jeopardy – I turned cold. Because I didn't share or understand how deep my pain went, they didn't and couldn't appreciate what it even meant for me to trust and be vulnerable with them. The value of my vulnerability was never measured because I never explained the cost. Once betrayed, I could not change my heart or my mind and turn back on the switch of vulnerability. It was a reminder that people are here to take advantage and only out for their own gain in some way. I kept a lot hidden and unsaid, which I now know was a mistake. But I also know that not everyone is meant to share in your pain and experiences. So there is a purpose for it all!

When I found out I was pregnant with my son, I was so depressed. Due to a prior procedure, I didn't think I could have any more children. My daughter was 12 and although I did want a son. I wanted a partner in life as well and in the current relationship, I was very far from being confident in thinking that could ever happen. So I cried, cried, prayed and cried as I did not want to repeat the same cycle from my daughter and become once again a single parent. Left to provide and survive on my own majority of the time. I had to eventually trust myself and my decision to go through with the pregnancy and accept the blessing of being able to have and provide for the child regardless of how the relationship may or may not work out. My decision was purely based on self-actualization and unlike my pregnancy with my daughter; I was in a position to stand on my own two feet; just me and the Creator, no opinions from my mother or anyone else. I had grown and learned to imperfectly trust my own instincts for my life. No matter all the mistakes I have made, the pain I have encountered, the lessons yet to be learned and the desire to be the best that I can be in this life.

I never had many boundaries until I reached the age of 29. Something happened for me when I was turning 30. It was like a light switch turned on to the "LIFE" mode to say put you first. No one will care about your mind, body, or your soul more than you do. Boundaries were something I lacked in my life with people and the capacity I allowed for them to impact my life through their actions. I started having uncomfortable conversations that I would HAVE never discussed in my early 20's with someone I was seeing. Ladies prior to getting intimate with someone, you MUST discuss and reveal your status in EVERY category. If that means going to the doctor together or showing one another your results thereafter, then so be it! But it is SO NECESSARY! Please hear me. Don't be afraid to be the one to lead the conversation, because it is your body, your life and NO one will care about it more than you and if you have slipped up and have made some mistakes – SO what, it's never too late to make it right for yourself and for the future. As long as you breathe – YOU can ALWAYS make a change. If he isn't willing to give you that comfort (i.e. go with you to the doctor etc) then please love yourself more than him, and reframe from being unprotected or putting yourself in a position to acquire something that is incurable. But don't disregard that the avoidance is a huge red, green, purple and blue FLAG waiving all the way from here to the Ivory Coast of Africa! So open you're EYES.

Finances are another uncomfortable conversation to have with someone you feel like there is a future with. How someone handles their bills is a huge indicator as to how they will handle the future bills should you decide to join households. Establish who has the better skill at being the CFO (Chief Financial Officer) in your home. Know where you are credit wise as it's never too late to get that back on track. I have heard some horror stories of folks going to the dealership with their partner all to discover that their credit worthiness is negative 0 and they owe thousands in child support. Don't be afraid to ask questions to know the person you are with and if you are unsure, ask for proof. The one you love and love you back will want to give you that comfort because they see the value in you and your relationship. Be prepared to give it back though, when it's needed. A Love given is love gained.

My parents have always been my example of love with 36 years of marriage and I still can't figure out all the way, HOW they do it. I question if I am capable of that kind of patience, trust, understanding and commitment. What is it that they found that I can't seem to find? Through it all I understand now that everyone's path, stages of learnings and purpose in life are different and mine is still being mapped out. Although I have made some astronomical mistakes, I believe that so long as I continue to want more for myself, I will have it. In my relationship journey, I became more aware of why I was attracting unhealthy relationships and holding on to them. I wrote down my goals instead of negative experiences and made that my form of release.

Knowing the Red Flags prior to getting into a relationship is critical to the success of said relationship. We all contribute something to the demise of a relationship – whether it was allowing someone to treat us horribly and not moving on, or knowing you should not have been with that person in the first place. You are quicker to recognize warning signs when you know what your boundaries are and what you need and want out of a relationship. Confusion is the biggest RED Flag of them all, which can be on both sides of the relationship. So know YOU and you will see sooner and clearer who is not what's best for you and have strength to walk away if needed. Never base your decision on what other people have to say, you will regret it later. Only you can determine how you feel and the course of your life. People love to judge – I know because I do it as well. People forget your pain when they are in theirs. It's a natural selfish human reaction that cycles from relationship to relationship and before you cherish the advice of someone else, do some self-analysis and determine how much you trust yourself and decisions. For whatever you believe in, ask for guidance and don't shun professional help either. We all have been damaged in some kind of way and its okay to talk about it.

Unexpectedly, I have found a love that is foreign to me and like no other that I have ever experienced and it has made me want to be a better woman, mother, sister, daughter and business women. Even though I fight against it sometimes due to fear and not being fully healed from my past, I know there is a beautiful future in sight because I am making steps to get that healing. With that, my love, mind and soul can only improve and I am excited about that. I am excited to be the best me for my children and to share that with a life partner. You can have what you desire, once you believe and keep moving forward which may eventually turn your Red Flags for STOP into Green for GO.

REFERENCES

[1] http://www.padv.org/documents/Statistics_DV.pdf

[2] http://www.safehorizon.org/index/what-we-do-2/domestic-violence--abuse-53/domestic-violence-the-facts-195.html

[3] http://www.padv.org/documents/Statistics_DV.pdf

[4] https://www.domesticshelters.org/domestic-violence-articles-information/faq/domestic-violence-statistics#.VZ8GWGfbJS4

112

CHAPTER 10

"I WANT TO DO WHAT YOU WANT TO DO!"

By

Aneitra Scott

Sacramento, CA

"I want to do what you want to do." I was so excited to hear these words! I have found a man that is really interested in doing what I like to do! Well, I want to go to church. I LOVE to go to church and I LOVE to worship the Lord! This is going to be great! If he loves to do what I want to he must be sent by God.

When we first met, he told me he wanted to do what I wanted to. We made small talk, but this is what stuck out the most. He didn't have much to say. I didn't mind, I just thought he was quiet and maybe a little shy. I shared with him that I went to church. I had two sons that I had been raising alone and my activities were centered around my children, the church and work. I wasn't actually looking to meet a man, and the fact that this man noticed me and showed interest in me was very exciting. He visited my church, met my friends and my Pastor. He started coming to church and mid-week Bible Study. He would sometimes beat me to church! He even joined the church, went to the New Membership Class and received his certificate and the right hand of fellowship from the church. Impressed? I was.

This thing, "I want to do what you want to do" seemed to be working out well. I was praising and thanking God for this man in my life. I was thanking and praising God for answering my prayers. Well, not quite! As time went on, and I needed this man to make a decision and I desired for him to take the lead, he wouldn't do it. I expected him to be able to handle business and make a decision and he couldn't do so. I was devastated. He put on a great show for me. He smiled real big and was very charming in the beginning. He pretended to be something he wasn't. He pretended to love the things I do to get close to me, but in reality, he was really looking for someone to take care of him.

What did I learn from him? Red Flag number one was his opening statement, "I want to do what you want to do!" I should have known something then. I grew up with brothers. I am an only girl. I have three brothers. I have more male uncles and cousins than I do females. Most of the men in my family are go getters. They get up and make a living for themselves. They don't sit around waiting for anyone to do anything for them, especially not a woman. They are responsible. They make decisions. They are leaders and they take care of their families. This is what I thought I was getting. What I missed was the detail of this man's true actions. In my mind, I got caught up in the fantasy of what a long term relationship could be. I pictured me planning out our future, vacations, finances, family events, a home and just about every other material thing to go along with that instead of listening to what he was saying or not saying.

What I should have been doing was asking him to make plans for us to go out and enjoy time with each other instead of me planning the dates. What I should have been doing was finding out how this man handled business. It was very hard for me to comprehend how he could, as a man, want to follow, instead of lead. It is okay for a woman to plan and make decisions and share her thoughts, ideas and dreams with a man. It is okay for a man to go along with a woman's plans too. If, however, the man is not capable of making any type of decision, at all, during a relationship, it is best for the woman to RUN! In the end, she will spare herself a lot of heartache and disappointment. "I want to do what you want to do," it's a trap!

"YOU SHOULD HAVE MADE ME LOVE YOU"

"You should have made me love you." He got caught cheating. Cheating occurred on a regular basis. The sad thing is that I would find out every time when the cheating occurred. I was never one to go through wallets, look through drawers, check pockets or go through cell phones to find out if I was being cheated on. God never let it sneak up on me or allowed me to hear I was being cheated on from any other source or any other person. I always found out because my man would leave the evidence out for me to see.

The cheating began with small things not adding up. Coming home late once a week and making an excuse that he was with his brother or hanging out with some of the guys after work. Once a week turned into to twice a week and twice a week turned into three times a week. Next came the excuse of, I'm working overtime on the weekends, and after work I am going to hang out with the guys so that's why I'm taking an extra pair of clothes, underwear and cologne. I'm raising my eyebrows now and thinking to myself, "Really?" My next thought, "I will wait to see the paycheck." The week of payday, he decides to pick an argument. This was to throw me off so I wouldn't ask about the money. We argue and we don't talk for a few days, and I have an, "I don't care," attitude. When payday arrives I don't see him until late, and of course, the money is gone. Late nights out and then came the phone calls all hours of the night. Isn't this what we do when we first meet that new person in our life? Next comes the overhearing of the conversations and me hearing, "You make me happy too, and I can't wait to see you." When you ask, "Who were you talking to?" The response is, "Oh that was my mother." You know better than that but now your mind is going. Your intuition starts kicking in and now you need proof so the snooping begins.

When I first began looking through my man's belongings I was devastated by my findings. I was so hurt and I was in disbelief behind what I found out. He told me he loved me and he was lying to me the whole time. When I confronted him about what I knew to be true, he lied. He lied even when I had proof. Then the day came and he told me, "You should have made me love you." I was so confused by his response. It didn't even make sense. I pleaded with him about how I took care of him, and how I was there for him, but it was like talking to a wall. Eventually, I made up mind that I was no longer going to be disrespected by this man. I did not have to take the, "Love" that he was giving. I left the relationship. It was the best thing I ever did! Red Flag Number Two – when a man tells you it is your responsibility to make you love him – it means he is actually cheating, he is already having conversations with another person, he lacks integrity and he wants to make you feel like it is your fault that the relationship did not work out. When this occurs, RUN! It is not your fault. There is nothing more for you to give.

I've learned a lot about relationships over the years. What I've learned the most is that, it takes courage to allow yourself to be vulnerable with another person because you have to trust, that they will not abuse your feelings and your emotions. When that trust is broken it takes courage to forgive that individual so you have the freedom to live a victorious life. Although I suffered many a broken heart, I am grateful for the wisdom I gained through the adversity. I am NOT bitter or broken. I am happy, healthy, whole, an overcomer, confident and wise.

PART III

The Twist

Now it wouldn't be right if we
didn't get at least one male's story?

"BALANCE"

By

Anonymous

Male, Age 46

Las Vegas, NV

I have had only a couple serious relationships. Just because we've been seeing each other for three weeks doesn't mean we're in a relationship. Most of my dating history revolved around hooking up and being able to do it again with no pressure. In my relationships, I was faithful. The one woman I thought was worthy of losing myself to, I let get away because I wasn't ready.

What I have learned from my personal experience and coaching others is balance. Now this word is often used but rarely practiced. Now it has different meanings but I will focus on the one that should be sought after when pursuing and maintaining a relationship; to bring into harmony or proportion.

This harmony and proportion or disproportion, starts at the very beginning. For example, I was in the comedy club one night with a few drinks in me. A nice looking woman walks by and her frame caught my attention so I talked to her and said "hey." She turned around, a quick conversation ensued and we met up later that week. We had a lot of conversation but no sex. Now at this point, I wasn't looking for a relationship neither was she.

We would see each other often and I had this wonderful plan where we did not need to be exclusive but use protection when away from each other (oh you thought I was going to try and make another person look bad. No! Sometimes it's you stupid). In the beginning, this piss poor plan was working, but of course it was the beginning! Anyway, I went out of town on business and during a phone conversation; the L Word came up! If only it had been the L word for lesbian. This instantly change the dynamics of the relationship for several reasons (but I will keep it short) 1) I didn't say it back, and 2) I questioned her sincerity and using those words.

Now it had only been a couple of months and for me, love isn't something you can give and take back. I don't say it unless I mean it out of respect for those I do that feel that way about and the dignity it carries. All the love is unconditional and it does come with obligations; otherwise it's meaningless. Anyways, we weren't there yet and that's what the short truth of why I didn't say it back. Foolish me, not only did I leave this woman out on a limb all by herself with love, I had the audacity to tell her to write down feelings; the pros and cons of why she loved me. The reason for this was because I knew she didn't really love me. Yeah that's me, not only do I know how I feel but I also know how you feel and why. Yes, arrogance is one of my traits too.

Now the relationship was off balance. At this point both parties want to assign blame either to justify their feelings or take the blame and try to return things to "normal." At that time in my life, I was and can still say I am a work in progress. An arrogant hardliner! She had messed up my good work talking about she loves me! Doesn't she know the importance I put on that word?

(Oh no) Why she doing this to me? (She's not "doing" anything to you, she's telling you how "she" feels!)

When I got back to town things were weird. I can't tell you how she felt but hurt and anger were probably two, and I was numb and confused. The conversations we had were strange because we did really like each other, but we were clearly on different pages. So we stopped seeing each other for a little while. This added up to about two months. When we started seeing each other again, we picked up where we left off but even stronger. I expressed some deeper feelings and so did she. It was just like the beginning, and that was one of the many problems. You see, we never fully addressed our differences well enough to move forward.

Having differences isn't the problem, its 1) where those differences are 2) are they the kind both parties can live with or get over, and 3) is anyone willing to change. The last one is the only one you have control over as to you, and is something you do to better yourself and the relationship; not something to make someone else happy.

These differences don't always bear themselves out in the beginning. It's the beginning! This is why it's so important to take your time even if they don't want to. You need time to see who you're dealing with meanwhile they get the same opportunity. This is dating while you're in or looking for a relationship, not just hooking up.

Looking back, I was saying "yes, let's see each other more because I do like having you around," but for her it was probably more like "this is it!" I want you now and forever! I'm only basing this on the actions that followed later because in less than three months she was pregnant (dun, dun, dun)! Yes, s*** just got real.

Now this brought a whole new set of problems to an already tenuous situation. I say tenuous because to me all relationships are by definition tenuous until hardships prove otherwise. Who she is or was as a person at that time has nothing to do with the fact that in my mind and by any reasonable account, we were not supposed to be bringing a child into the world at "that" time together.

At the time we had known each other for less than a year. In fact it had been only about nine months, four of which we had spent apart. There was no talk of marriage, we did not live together, and she already had seven year old son that needed more than a "little" consideration. There had been a discussion about any possible pregnancy prior to this. Before becoming pregnant she said she would have an abortion. Once she got pregnant, she changed. She gave me a number of reasons why, but long story short she just "couldn't" have an abortion. I would later come to understand and more than appreciate this later (I love her for it). Meanwhile, I was angry, pissed, stressed, confused, and more than a little panicked. She lied! She was changing our (most importantly mine) lives. We ain't ready for this, why is she doing this to us, most importantly me?

I threw many stones at that woman at the start; it's embarrassing to think of who I was then. Yes she did lie and change her mind, but I gave her the chance to do that. Who didn't wear a condom? Me, that's who! As mad as I was at her, I was ten times as mad at myself for not taking control over the one thing that I know I had complete control over, me!

For the first four months, I pouted and pissed on her apparent happiness and unexplained joy she seemed to be getting from this whole pregnancy experience. I still wanted an abortion, (yeah a real a**hole). You see, that wasn't apparent on the surface that I had/have trust issues and her change of heart, lie, or whatever you want to call it only exasperated these deep seeded feelings to no end.

Eventually, our issues still unresolved, we moved forward. About six months into her pregnancy, I moved in. Everything was good and we both wanted a healthy mom and baby. Things aren't perfect but they were far from the place they had been, and four months later we had the most beautiful baby boy known to mankind.

I always wanted a wife before children. Even though I wasn't a husband, I still wanted to be a good dad, a father. At this point she was the mother of my child, not my "baby mama." Our son allowed us to work on one accord for a while. It was a short while. Sooner rather than later, the mother of my child needed me to not just love her but to be "in love" with her. Personally (since you're talking about me), I've always been circumspect, a little hesitant if not all out distrustful when it comes to being "in love" especially when it comes to a man being "in love" with a woman.

There's no science to back me, but I have come to believe that it is best for a woman (man) to seek a man who loves and respects her.

To have a man or woman who is in love with you can lead to some dangerous situations and outcomes. Some would probably explain those situations of obsession or possessiveness. They may be right, but the person acting that way would talk about how "in love," they were. Besides, what argument can you have to being loved and respected? I can still disrespect you in the bedroom when you need or want it.

Anyway, I just couldn't tell her I was "in love" with her because I didn't feel that way and I didn't think she was "in love" either. I needed answers, real tangible proof. I just can't trust your feelings and emotions because they change. I had never told a woman I was in love with her either. As stated already, I didn't really trust that. On the other hand, she had these feelings and emotions before, even planned a child and delivered that promise with someone else she was "in love" with. She had already had that previous six year relationship in which at some point you told them you were "in love" with them too. So my question was what makes me any different?

Don't crucify me yet, we had some good times to. I wasn't always so difficult to deal with. In fact, for all the problems I saw at the time (some real fun and some imagined) there was one that concerned her the most. Security! Now she never said this word when we talked about it but it was truly one of the things she wanted most. Oddly enough, I felt the same in that I ask myself a question (not consciously) "Is this a person that I can (and will) trust with all my heart (and life)? But before we get to that answer, breaking news pregnancy number two! No, I'm serious!

In my world, babies and small children are loved period. All of mine are going to get that from me unequivocally. Not just because I'm supposed to, but because they deserve it. My family is the same way, we are far from perfect, but we are very loving. So 14 months after the birth of my first child, we welcomed the new most beautiful baby girl known to mankind.

With two babies in less than two years, a significant amount of pressure was put on me to be in love (well duh). But as for me, I was concerned I was already deeply in love with the only people I trusted with it, my kids. I quickly came to realize that relationship with my kids would suffer if things continue down the same path. Also, I did love her (my baby momma), so I decided to give things a possible chance at success.

There were some things that needed to be cleaned up in my life on a personal level. So I set a time limit to be done with those things, about six months, and focus more on any and all positive things in my life; most importantly my children and their mother.

In my mind, if the difference between us having a happy life and being in love, was me! I would change the selfish parts of me to give that a chance. I was the only one I had control over. Anyway, if she's true, she will be; if she ain't, she won't be. Besides going back to school to give my business plan a better chance at success makes a good decision. Slowing down on alcohol makes me all around better person. Being fully committed in words and deeds (the words that were lacking) to her and my kids make for happier life for us all.

But what's that saying "men plan while God laughs?" Well I don't know if he was laughing at me or disappointed, but some unforeseen circumstances blew everything up. Love proved to be less than its claim because when it could have been put into action and show up, it was absent.

Now all this started with 'me' telling 'you' all about how to pursue and maintain balance while in or pursuing a relationship (ha); and just like relationships I've been all over the place. But that's just it; matters of the heart don't often reap rational decisions. That's normal, but you just can't stay in an irrational state with unreasonable expectations of the other person or yourself. But it is important to know what you want and where you're looking for it. Balance ain't so much what you're reaching for but what you are standing on.

So build a solid foundation under yourself. This has less to do with not caring what anybody thinks and more about caring about what's important. While doing that, know that you are worth getting to know and so is (or should) anyone you desire to be with. When you truly decide to be in a relationship with someone, there is loyalty and obligations that come along with that. You both have a responsibility to nurture that. No one person can carry the responsibility of the relationship by themselves though one or both may be called upon to do so for a time. That's love, that's real, that's life! Remember that song "Lean On Me?" Yeah!

Once the two of you have established a solid foundation with each other together and you have are true to it, if that person goes off the reservation for 'any' reason or 'whatever' reason, that has nothing to do with you. You are not to blame, it ain't your fault. If you forgive, forgive; if you don't, then don't. Don't blame yourself! Your love is a reflection of 'you' and theirs a reflection of them. My love can influence, but it is not the arbitrator of another person's actions. My love (though I'm not always) is patient, kind, caring, forgiving, and fearless among other things. What is yours? We don't have to be exactly alike for are attributes of love to match up.

You can't just push through what you want and think just because you really 'like' someone means you love them. In fact, you probably don't even 'like' them; you just like how they make you feel. Love doesn't conform us, we give ourselves to it. Life is a beautiful mess and relationships can be the dirtiest part, but it's the ways they clean us up that is important and should be celebrated.

As for my story, it's not over, but I am available. My kids are my best gifts and I wouldn't trade them for the world. They are the best part of the world and inspire me to be a better person. Now that's love!

PART IV

I wanted to touch on some of the different types of men I have come in contact with or observed over the course of my life. These are the various types of men who usually are the ones to exhibit Red Flags. Some men may fit into one or more of these categories.

(By Shamay Speaks)

The "Situation" Man:

The Situation Man may tell you things like, "I am in a situation that goes something like this:"

- I stay with my ex but we're broke up and I am still on the lease, so I have to stay here and pay my part of the rent until the lease ends.

- I stay with my ex and we've been broken up, we sleep in separate rooms, but I have to stay here until we sell our house.

- I stay with my baby's mothers and we have been unhappy for a while. I am only there for my kids.

- I am trying to get things in order so I can leave but my kid's mother is crazy, and I don't want her to start playing games with my kids.

- It's just complicated or it's just a complicated "situation."

- I can't afford a divorce because she will take everything.

The "Take All The Milk But Not Buy The Cow" Man:

This man will allow you to give him your all but he won't commit. Meaning that he will take all the milk (you and all you have to offer) with no intentions on buying the cow (the cow being you and a committed relationship). Examples of giving him your milk: giving him your time, your heart, your body, and maybe even your money. There's an old saying, "Why buy the cow if you get all the milk free?"

The "Doesn't Close One Chapter Before Reading A New One" Man:

This man is similar to the Situation Man because he's technically with someone else. He tells you he's confused because he loves you both, and you may feel like you can help him decide. This type of man is not ready to fully close the door on his last situation/relationship and unless you want an open relationship, you may want to run the other way.

The Liar By Omission Man:

The Liar by Omission Man is the man who appears to be honest and genuine and will even tell you how trustworthy he is. His definition of honesty is only telling the truth about what you may want to hear. If you ever accuse him of lying, he will say he didn't lie because he just didn't tell you or because you never asked. He makes it appear that the reason you didn't know his secret was due to your lack of knowledge or lack of inquiry.

The "Father Of The Year Who Never Gets To See His Kid(s)" Man:

The father of the year, who never gets to see his kid(s), may say things like this:

- My kid's mother is always causing drama because she's bitter.

- My kid's mother won't let me see my kids, simply because we're not together.

- My kid's mother hasn't got over our break up so she just wants to make my life miserable, and if she knows I am with you; it will cause too many problems.

The above reasons are typically his excuse for why you haven't met his children yet. From my observations and experience, this type of man is usually still in a relationship with his children's mother or he just may be a dead beat dad.

The "In-Between" Man:

The In-Between man is usually holding onto a woman who won't put up with his "ways" while he's with a woman who will; furthermore, he will continue to string the other woman along.

The "Damaged" Man:

The damaged man may say things like:

- My ex cheated on me so I can't trust women and so I am scared to commit.

- I like the way things are and I don't want to ruin it because it happened to me before.

- I was a good dude until I got played and cheated on.

The "Plant Many Seeds But NEVER Grow A Garden" Man:

The plant many seeds but NEVER grow a garden guy is the man who has over three children with three or more different women. None of these women were ever his wife either. Planting seeds basically means a man who never likes to use protection and doesn't care how many kids he has because he has no intentions on making a family. You see, that's where the family "growing a garden" comes in. Typically he's never been in a serious relationship with most of his children's mothers.

The "Lust" Man (He's amazing in the bedroom):

The lust man is the man who is amazing in the bedroom. He can make you feel as if nothing else in the world exists in those moments. He tells you that you're the only one he gives extra pleasure to. This is the type of man that will cause you to play with your own mind. The intimacy is so good; you start confusing lust for love. He may really make you feel as if he's looking for love. This kind of man typically causes your mind to play tricks on you or cause you to go against your better judgment.

"I Don't Like Labels" Man:

The "I don't like labels" man is the man who has every reason not to put a label on your "relationship." He may say things like:

- I just got out of a relationship and I am trying to take things slow.

- Why can't we just see where this goes?

- I know we've been seeing each other for six months but I am not ready for a commitment.

- Why can't we just continue with how things are because labels messes things up.

- I am still young and just wanna have fun. I don't want to be tied down but I like where things are going so you never know.

- I am not dating anyone else but I am not ready for labels, we should give it more time.

The "Rationalize" Man:

He does things the make you try to rationalize his odd behavior. You may find yourself making excuses for his odd behavior, leading you to ignore the red flags.

"The One Legged" Man:

This type of man is the one who has never had anything of his own without his mother or a woman. This type of man usually lives at home and probably has only moved out when it was with a woman. Nine times out of ten, the woman he moves out with is the breadwinner. So basically, he only stands on one leg alone but needs a woman to stand on his own two feet. This kind of man usually likes a woman to be his rescuer or "sugar mama".

The "Predator Man" aka "Sugar Mama" Man:

The predator man is the man who doesn't have much going for himself but he's looking for an established woman. He usually targets women who are independent like women who have a good job, good credit, their own place, car, etc. This type of man usually doesn't have many goals and may stay at home with his parents or his mama. He will usually do just enough to wheel you into falling for him then all his financial dilemmas will start and he needs some support from you. He usually never has steady work and a "good excuse" why he doesn't.

The "Lonely Predator" Man:

This man is similar to the predator man but he intentionally seeks out woman who are feeling lonely and haven't had a man in a while. He tells you exactly what you want to hear most of the time until he gets what he wants. He plays on your emotions especially if he feels that you may be desperate for love.

The "BUT" Guy:

The "But" guy always seems great and if you were telling your friends about him, it would go something like this:

- "Girl, I met this man and he was fine! He has a nice car, a job, and is so sweet. But he has five kids with four women."

- "Girl, I met this guy at the store the other day and he was so nice. He has one child and is looking for a wife; BUT he lives with his Mama."

- "Girl, I met this great man, but he's in the middle of a divorce. He still lives with his wife because of the kids but they sleep in separate rooms."

The "I Am The Star In My Very Own Fiction Movie and I Love To Bring Along Blind Co-Stars AKA the Sociopath" Man:

This man is the man who usually lives so many lives and tells so many lies that he actually believes them because he lives them on a daily basis. He is very charismatic and quite charming or down to earth. Everyone in town who knows him, would describe him as a very cool person. Remember these types of men are stars in their own movies and they bring along blind female co-stars, meaning the women involved are usually blind sided when the truth is revealed. He can be considered a sociopath when it comes to relationships.

The "Persistent" Man:

The man who has been that friend for years but he just may be the one! The persistent man is generally a good man by definition. Be sure to truly consider the true reason you never gave him a chance, is it because you're so used to "bad boys" or you are just not interested.

The "Dilemma" Man:

The "Dilemma" man always has a "situation" or problem that he needs your "support" to solve. He always has an issue whether it's at work or with family and he needs your "support." He's usually in-between jobs and needs your help because he's "trying." He talks, a very good talk, about his plans yet there is always some sort of problem in his life. He usually in a "situation" that causes him to need to "borrow" money and/or come "stay" with you.

Note: Some men may fall into one or more of the categories. Take time to observe when you are dating. Observe actions and words with actions that follow.

The Take Away

(Epilogue)

By

Shamay Speaks

The "Take Away" because it all starts and ends with YOU!

I went back and forth with myself as to how to end the book like how to effectively break down the take away, so I decided to break it down in questions, explanations, and examples. I decided this because I think us as women; forget to ask ourselves these questions. The real question is do we know the answers ourselves? These questions definitely require some soul searching which can sometimes require you to confront questions and answers about yourself that you may not want to answer or know the answer to. Sometimes we may not be mentally or spiritually ready for the answers. I have found that most of the time you have to be in a good place in life to deal with answers to questions like this.

(Note: *I am going to be very candid and honest with these REAL questions, explanations, and examples. These questions are meant to be thought provoking)*

1. To be ready for any relationship, you have to work on yourself first. The first relationship you have is with you. Ask yourself are you really happy with you? Have you fell

in love with you or do you enjoy your own company? These are definitely questions to consider when you feel ready to date and enter a relationship especially after getting over past hurts. According to this anonymous quote I found on Instagram, its states, "The enjoyment of being single while not looking or caring about having or not having a significant other. Enjoying quiet time of your own thoughts. Making yourself smile. Cooking for yourself. Loving who you are and who you are becoming." You have to be happy with you to be happy with anyone else because it all starts and ends with you.

2. If you are not happy, do you really know why? Are you even ready to confront the why? Have you ever truly thought about what happiness means and looks like to you? Sometimes being happy is a learned illusion. For example, a woman may go from one cheater to another but rationalize in her mind, that the second is better than the first because he treats her better; moreover, you stay in this relationships because you tell yourself no one is "perfect" and its "love," right? Another example is, a lot of people go from one toxic relationship to another because a few things are slightly better and rationalize things like we may yell and argue a lot but he doesn't put his hands on me. After doing things like this for so long eventually you lose sight of what you really want from all the times you may have settled; in essence, it can cause you to lose sight of your core values. Some people feel that money can buy happiness in a relationship but all the money in the world can't give you your core values. Core values come from within because it all starts and ends with you.

3. Ask yourself, how you do view love? Do you ever truly soul search and wonder where your past and current perception of love comes from? Has your perception changed or is it the same? Does it come from past relationships, your parents, TV, family or lack thereof? When you start to think about this, you're mixed feelings, past toxic relationships including how you were raised; may start to kick in. You may think you never seen "love" modeled but even if you feel you haven't had "true" love but you have had relationships; I am sure you are probably aware of what love is not just by knowing how you felt if you were mistreated in a relationship especially if you were cheated on or abused. Do you remember that love is actually an action word? Love is displayed through ones actions and how their actions make you feel inside. Actions of love are supposed to make you feel good and nothing less. Some of us may have grown up in an abusive home so we may think that abuse is part of love or that it's normal. One thing that must be stressed is that abuse is not love whether it is verbal, emotional, or physical abuse; intentional mistreatment in any form will never equal love. As the old saying goes, "Love doesn't hurt" but this depends on what your perception of what love is; moreover only you know your internal definition of love because it all starts and ends with you!

4. Do you trust your intuition? This is your red flag alarm. Do you continue to get in situation-ships or relationships when you know that deep down inside, you have a bad feeling about it? Your intuition will never steer you wrong. It's always been said century after century, your intuition will never steer you wrong. I honestly feel intuition is

comparable to being warning signs from God but depends on your perception because it all starts and ends with you!

5. Do you know you're worth/your value? Do you feel you have self worth? Do you know what you deserve in a life especially in relationships? Have you ever been mistreated in a relationship and said "I don't deserve this?" If you have ever had that feeling in a relationship then that is a sign of what you will and will not accept because it will compromise your self-worth. A good man can understand and appreciate a woman's worth and he won't ask you to discount your self worth to appease him or treat you as such. Compromising your self worth may be a deal breaker for you but only you can decide what your deal breakers are because it all starts and ends with you!

6. Are you dating with boundaries and standards? Boundaries can also help shape your standards. Boundaries protect your heart because not everyone deserves your heart. Are you jumping head first into relationships without taking time to see if they even fit your core values? For example, are you being intimate on the first date and mistaking good loving for real romantic chemistry? Where are the boundaries in doing this? How will he know what your boundaries are if you haven't set your own standards? You must have standards but not so many that you block love by being too picky. Set your Boundaries and make sure you have standards because they run together. Remember no one, but you, will know your boundaries or standards because it all starts and ends with you.

7. **This a real question that we may not want to answer within ourselves** Are you saving yourself for someone you can establish a deeper emotional connection with before intimacy? Or are you going with the flow when dating and giving yourself too soon without a commitment yet your core values are to be married one day? Do you have reasonable expectations when considering giving yourself to someone too soon? For example, if you want a man with no strings attached, then you shouldn't think it will turn to love because deep down, you know sex doesn't equal love. Many of us mistake lust for love. If all you want is a sex partner then, be sure to protect yourself and your body. Never make the mistake of assuming that a no-commitment friend will be father of the year when all he wanted was no string intimacy. Believing this will more than likely earn you a lifetime headache, even though a child is a blessing in disguise; having a child will create a lifelong connection to someone you really don't know or want to continue to know. If you want a husband then make sure you are not giving all of you before a commitment, and giving all of you includes your body. If you want a husband, wait and get to know him before becoming intimate. I say this because if you're desire is to be married then no commitment intimacy wouldn't be aligned with your core values of finding a husband. We have to have reasonable expectations if we want happiness not heartache. Your actions should match your desires but only you know your true desires for your love life because it all starts and ends with you.

8. Do you move fast when dating? Do you go on three or four dates and feel like you already know that person? Do you

feel like intimacy means that you know someone better even though you don't truly know them? Keep in mind, things that start quick end quick. Don't move too fast no matter how tempting it may be. Just think about it, if you were car shopping, wouldn't you make sure the car has everything you want like all the bells and whistles? This means to need to take time to know if that person is what you want. It has been said that each time you give your body to someone, you leave a piece of your soul with them. I know that's deep but really reflect on that. For those that are mothers with daughters, just think of what you will tell your daughter about giving her body too soon, etc. Be sure your actions align with the advice you would give your daughter even if you made mistakes in the past. Take your time! Things that are truly meant to be will be and only time can reveal if that person is meant for you. There is where that famous Steve Harvey 90 day rule comes in; however, it has been said that it can take a minimum of 2 years of truly get to know someone. Moving too fast can cause you to overlook some red flags. Some red flags can take longer than others to reveal themselves. Don't cloud your logical judgment for your life, just because someone can make you feel good and shows you attention. Ultimately, don't be reckless with your heart or your body; guard them like a safe. Only you can know from your own experiences and observations whether you move too fast or not because it all starts and ends with you!

9. Do you take time between relationships to analyze the pros and cons from your past relationships? Some of us may definitely need more time than others depending on how bad the past relationships were. When you meet someone

new take even more time. I totally agree with Steve Harvey's 90 day rule as I mentioned before. Think deep how many times some of us have not waited 90 days and today, we are not in any of those past relationships where we didn't wait. I know it has been said that the best way to get "over" someone is to date someone new and that may work for SOME people; however, I disagree. I feel that hopping in relationships to fast without healing from past hurts, doesn't do anything but put a bandage on things; and that bandage will present itself in the form of baggage. Give yourself time alone give time to gain clarity to deal with unresolved issues. Some of us may even need additional support like counseling to help us work through internal issues. Don't ever allow anyone to make you feel bad for seeking additional support! New people can't heal old wounds from past relationships, this is only something you can do because it all starts and ends with you!

10. How do you allow others to treat you? One of the most honest things I have heard is that we teach people how to treat us. I agree that we teach people how to treat us in every relationship in life when dating, relationships, and even with family. If you want love and respect then be sure you are not constantly allowing others, especially men, to disrespect you and what you stand for. Disrespecting you by treating you as if you don't deserve respect, love, and loyalty. Learn what your individual core values are when it comes to how you feel you should be treated. Following your heart is where your core values start but only you know what these values mean to you because it all starts and ends with you!

147

11. Do you understand what it means to have self-awareness? Do you understand your own wants, needs, bad choices, and habits? Just like us as people bring awareness to causes in this world, we as individuals have to bring awareness to our own true wants, needs, and desires in relationships and life. The red flags will slowly become more visible as your self-awareness rises, lining up with your core values. Boundaries also tie into self-awareness. If you don't know what you'll tolerate from having self-awareness, how will you know what you're boundaries are? Self- awareness will help you understand when its time to walk away from a relationship. It has been said that only you know when you have had enough of an unhealthy relationship. Friends and family can tell you their thoughts and/or opinions but ultimately it all starts and ends with you!

12. Are you accountable for your choices? Do you take ownership and responsibility for your choices in relationships? Or do you just blame the other person and become the victim? For example, like that old saying goes, "fool me once, shame on you; fool me twice, shame on me." It's definitely not your fault if you were in a relationship and someone cheated on you or mistreated you but your reactions and responses are your responsibility. When you decide, for whatever reason, to stay in an unhealthy relationship; you must be accountable and take ownership for your choice to stay. Yes, some things are easier said then done but things are definitely not as hard when you have self-awareness, self-worth, boundaries, standards, realistic expectations, and take time to gain clarity between relationships. We all make mistakes but we must learn to be accountable, embrace the outcome of a

situation (whether favorable to us or not), and move forward. It has been said by TD Jakes, "You can't deal with what you won't confront." Be sure you confront your issues before you get into new relationships. Only you know what issues you may need to confront because it all starts and ends with you!

The real question that remains is if we know the answers to these questions, what are we going to do about it? I would like to say that I definitely hope you enjoyed the book as well as I hope you were able to gain insight. I hope you were able to learn something about yourself to help you change your dating style to get more effective results. As I mentioned in the book, what always sticks in my head is when I think of what I want in a relationship and what my core values are, is when my Big Ma told me, "Why buy the cow, if you get all the milk FREE?" I was actually a teenager when she first said this to me and I didn't think much of it but now, in my 30's, it makes complete sense. I don't think I was ready to receive the message my Big Ma was giving me. Ask yourself are you giving all of you without a commitment? It's giving a man all of you: mind, body, and soul without him earning it or making a commitment. Are you giving all the milk away without him buying the cow? Let that question marinate in your mind for a few minutes then think about your past or current relationships or situation-ships when answering this question. (My definition of a situation-ship is a "relationship," that lacks a verbally mutual understanding between two people). If so, how often have you gave away your milk? Have you done this so much it's become natural for you; although, each time there are more signs that this person is not who you see in your future? Sometimes we can give so much of ourselves away that we lose sight of what we stand for meaning that we can lose sight of our core values. I remember telling myself as a teenager that I didn't want to have kids until marriage and I would say this was a core value of mine; however, my actions were not following my core values. I was losing myself within my own actions and my actions were not aligned with my dating style. I truly thought I had it all together but why was I so consumed in chasing what I didn't want. I loss sight of what my core values were. I thought I had it all together and I loved me but why was I giving away my milk as my Big Ma said? It seemed like each time I would give away my milk being all of me to an unworthy man; I would lose more of myself little by little. One of my favorite songs is "Trouble" Tyler Swift says, "I don't think you know who you are until you lose who you are." I lost so much of me that I lost sight of what I wanted out of relationships and I lost what I stood for in relationships. I think it's very easy to lose yourself in a relationship when you don't know yourself and you lose sight of what you deserve. I have been through so much, maybe not as much as some, but I had to learn the hard way that I could no longer date without having self-awareness, self-worth, boundaries, standards, realistic expectations, and taking the appropriate time to gain clarity between relationships. I now take time to get to know who I date and I protect my heart by also protecting my body because I eventually want marriage. I truly feel God will only give you so many signs before he has to give you a lesson so you can learn to align your core values with your dating style; but most importantly learning and believing your worth. I am now fully accountable for my bad choices in relationships and I can take ownership for my choice to stay in unhealthy relationships. If I kept up my bad dating patterns, true love will miss me because I would be too busy pulling off all the damaged layers of hurt from my past relationships. I no longer have damaged layers also known as Baggage. No matter if we go through 2 or 20 relationships, if you don't deal with YOU; you will keep getting the relationships you don't want. "The definition of insanity is doing the same thing over and over and expecting different results." (Benjamin Franklin) I was getting the same results until I took ownership over my choices and learned to love me. There is so much beauty in being able to say I have learned from my past and I love me more than ever. I do not blame the past men I dated nor do I harbor guilt, I just continue to move forward with self-awareness, self-worth, boundaries, standards, realistic expectations, and clarity.

Sarah Jakes, hit the nail on the head, she said, "Give him a better version of you!" Everyone is different but I still want and believe in marriage, and I want to be able to give my husband the best me. I could go on and on but the moral of the story is that it all starts with you. It starts with you following your heart and your CORE values you envision for your future especially in relationships.

This book is designed to help other women follow their heart, gain self awareness, learn from past mistakes, and truly discover themselves. Look back at your past choices, soul search, and start the better version of you from today forward. My ultimate goal for this book is for the book to, as Tyler Perry nicely put it, "Be a point of light for someone!" I hope my story as well all the amazing women and men, who shared their stories; will shine some light in your life. Our relationship choices will either drain you or enhance your spirit but God has the power to turn a mess into a message. I am a firm believer that when the student (you) is ready, the teacher (tools and self awareness) will appear; therefore, it's about YOU and what YOU want. Be the best you- Mind, Body, and Soul!

Stay blessed, keep the faith, trust God, and pray daily! May God bless everyone who took the time to purchase and read this book. Thank you!

About the Author
Shamay Speaks

Tanicia Currie is a single mother with a full time job, who does not believe in settling in life. Having faced many life challenges including having three heart surgeries in just 32 years, Tanicia feels that God definitely gave her a purpose.

Growing up in a challenging environment with a drug addiction in her home, she convinced herself that there had to be more to life than those circumstances. Rather than allow her upbringing to dictate her success, she decided to turn her life's hardships into motivation to persevere in life.

 She became the first in her immediate family to graduate college with a Bachelor's degree. In 2009, she later went on to opening Cause' N A Stir Entertainment hosting events from concerts to fashion shows to annual toy drives. Her life changed in 2013 when her daughter Laniyah was born. Laniyah is the best blessing she received but this also showed her that it was time to kick life into over drive. In 2014, she decided to finish her book she started over eight years ago. She published her first book titled "Deep Within I Knew He Wasn't for Me," October 2015. She is also a featured author in "Igniting The Vision," released on September 26, 2015. Shamay is passionate about empowering others to rise above their circumstances and take charge of their destiny.

Tanicia's mission in life is to chase all that life has to offer, never give up, and stay humble. Tanicia truly hopes to use her life story, book, videos, and speaking to inspire others to follow their dreams despite their circumstances.

Subscribe to Shamay's Channel:

www.Youtube.com/ShamaySpeaks

Follow Shamay:

www.facebook.com/ShamaySpeaks
Instagram and Twitter @ShamaySpeaks

Email: ShamaySpeaks@gmail.com

Website: www.shamayspeaks.com

www.ingramcontent.com/pod-product-compliance
Lightning Source LLC
Chambersburg PA
CBHW072013040426
42447CB00009B/1614